THE COMPLETE DEBT RELIEF MANUAL

Step-By-Step Procedures for:
Budgeting, Paying Off Debt, Negotiating Credit Card and IRS Debt Settlements, Avoiding Bankruptcy, Dealing with Collectors and Lawsuits, and Credit Repair - Without Debt Settlement Companies

JOHN OSWALD

authorHOUSE®

AuthorHouse™
1663 Liberty Drive
Bloomington, IN 47403
www.authorhouse.com
Phone: 1-800-839-8640

© 2013 John Oswald. All Rights Reserved.

No part of this book may be reproduced, stored in a retrieval system, or transmitted by any means without the written permission of the author.

Published by AuthorHouse 01/03/2013

ISBN: 978-1-4772-9756-8 (sc)
ISBN: 978-1-4772-9755-1 (hc)
ISBN: 978-1-4772-9754-4 (e)

Library of Congress Control Number: 2012923415

Any people depicted in stock imagery provided by Thinkstock are models, and such images are being used for illustrative purposes only. Certain stock imagery © Thinkstock.

This book is printed on acid-free paper.

Because of the dynamic nature of the Internet, any web addresses or links contained in this book may have changed since publication and may no longer be valid. The views expressed in this work are solely those of the author and do not necessarily reflect the views of the publisher, and the publisher hereby disclaims any responsibility for them.

DISCLAIMER

The author is not an attorney. Nothing in this book should be considered legal, accounting, or professional advice. If legal or other professional advice is required, the author recommends seeking competent legal or professional advice. Though this information is meant to be accurate and helpful, and many people may achieve wonderful results through the use of this information, including breaking free from debt and saving thousands of dollars in the process, no guarantees of positive results, or avoidance of negative results, are being promised or guaranteed by the author. Certain situations carry inherent risk, such as representing yourself in a lawsuit. The author makes no guarantees of success, and the user of this information assumes all risks and potential liabilities involved.

Introduction

This book is not only about getting out of debt. This book shows you how to:

- Decide on the best way to eliminate your debt and then DO IT
- Handle Creditors
- Handle lawsuits
- Protect or repair your credit report and score
- Save money while doing all the above

At the end of this book are check lists you can use to keep track of your actions and progress. Please make copies and use them as you go through this process.

Most of this information is kept secret by creditors, debt settlement companies, and attorneys. All of them are after one thing – your money. If they told you what I'm about to tell you, they would go out of business.

In assembling this information through personal experience, I spent thousands of dollars on a debt settlement company, accountants, attorneys, and interest on my debt. This book is a roadmap I wish I would have had a few years ago. I could have easily saved several hundred times the price you paid for this information, and, if you're in a similar situation, and you use the tools you're about to learn, you will too.

I want you to keep your money. I want you out of debt. I want America out of debt. And I want the word to spread. Please share what you learn from this book.

In order for this process to work, you have to decide right now that debt is your enemy and that you want to beat it. You will need to stay the course and stand strong against pressure from creditors, collection agencies, attorneys, fear, and the temptation to keep spending money you don't have. You can get out of debt and stay out. You can rebuild your credit and improve your credit score. You can even recover from bankruptcy if that is your only option. And I am about to show you how.

Table of Contents

Introduction vii

Chapter 1 - The Problem: Slavery to Debt 1
    Types of Debt 3
    Good News - you can get out of debt and stay out 3

Chapter 2 - The Secrets 5
    Credit Card Company Secrets 5
    Debt Settlement Company Secrets 7
    Collection Agency Secrets 9
    IRS Secrets 10
    Debt Collection Attorney Secrets 12

Chapter 3 - Which Debt Elimination Strategy Should You Use? 15
    Making Minimum Payments 16
    Consolidation 16
    Roll up 16
    Settlement 17
    Bankruptcy 19
    Endless Collections and Lawsuits 21
    Debt Elimination Strategy Decision Tool 22

Chapter 4 - The Almighty Budget 23
    Discretionary spending 25
    Saving an Emergency Fund 26

Chapter 5 - How to Create a Budget 27
    Example Budget Spreadsheet 31

Chapter 6 - How to Cut Up Your Credit Cards 32

Chapter 7 - How to Eliminate Debt by Roll Up 33

Chapter 8 - How to Eliminate Debt by Settlement 35
    Example Settlement Offer From Creditor. 41
    Example Letter for Settlement Offer. 42
    Example Letter for Countering a Creditor's Settlement Offer 43
    Example Letter for Acceptance of Settlement (conditional). 44
    Example Letter for Acceptance of Settlement 45

Chapter 9 - How I Eliminated My Debt by Bankruptcy (without an attorney) 46

Chapter 10 - How to Eliminate IRS Debt 50
    Options for Repaying the IRS 50

Chapter 11 - How to Deal with Creditors and Collection Agencies. . . . 53
    Example Cease and Desist Letter 58
    Example Cease and Desist AND Debt Validation Letter to Collection Agency 59
    Example Debt Validation Letter to Collection Agency 60

Chapter 12 - How I Dealt with a Creditor Lawsuit (without an Attorney) 61
    Copy of Lawsuit Filed Against Me (4 pages) 69
    Here is Roughly How I Would Answer Today. 73
    Copy of Chase's Reply to My Bogus (original) Affirmative Defenses. 76
    Statute of Limitations by State (years). 77

Chapter 13 - How to Repair Your Credit Report. 78
    Example Letter to Collector to Remove Inquiries. 84
    Example Letter to Credit Bureau to Remove Inquiries. 85
    Example Letter to Credit Bureau (or Collector) to Request Correction to Credit Report. 86

Chapter 14 - How to Rebuild Your Credit 88

Chapter 15 - To Your Freedom (Staying out of Debt) 93

Chapter 16 - The Checklists. 95
    BUDGET CHECKLIST. 96
    DEBT ROLL UP CHECKLIST 97
    DEBT *SETTLEMENT* CHECKLIST 98
    John's BANKRUPTCY CHECKLIST 100

Chapter 1 - The Problem: Slavery to Debt

If you're reading this book, you are probably struggling to pay your mortgage and loan payments, medical bills, taxes, insurance, etc.

> *The rich rules over the poor, and the borrower becomes the lender's slave* —Proverbs 22:7
> *King Solomon*

You may be desperate enough to pay an attorney or debt consolidation firm to help you fight lawsuits or negotiate settlements with the credit card companies or other creditors. Or maybe you've already paid someone a bunch of money for help, only to be frustrated by continued phone calls from creditors, Sheriffs serving you court summonses, and your shrinking bank balance.

One of the wisest men of all time likened being in debt to being a slave. Debt is a cruel master. Debt kills - marriages, careers, retirements, and dreams, even though the knuckleheads in the federal government would tell you otherwise. Overspending causes debt, and debt is BAD.

In multiple studies, debt and financial issues stand alone as the top reason for divorce.

In fact, at the end of my first marriage, I had cashed out my 401K (over $150K), which caused me to owe the IRS a hefty sum (over $24K), bought a home I couldn't afford, bought a boat I couldn't afford, bought a new car I couldn't afford, and had around $100K in unsecured debt, mainly credit cards.

While separated, I paid the mortgage, all the bills, the boat payment, her car payments, and child support. I used credit cards to buy food, clothes, gas, etc.

In the mean-time, I had paid my divorce attorney several thousand dollars, *by credit card*. My attorney, it turns out, didn't do anything for me I couldn't have done better, for myself, if I had known then what I know now. There is a chapter in this book about my experience representing myself in court. It's not for everyone, but it can be done.

And how did I deal with that $24K IRS debt? I paid as much as I could *on credit cards*. The IRS actually recommends doing this to avoid their steep fees and penalties.

At that point my cards were maxed out and I couldn't get another card. I heard an advertisement on the radio about a debt settlement company. Once again, in my ignorance and desperation, I spent thousands of dollars for help with something I could have done myself, *for free*.

The debt settlement company (I'll call them "settlers" from now on.) recommended I stop all credit card payments at once and start saving around $634/month in a new savings account. For the first six months, they took over $400 of that $634, and put it in their pockets. They promised to deal with the creditors for me and negotiate settlements when the time was right.

The credit card companies kept calling. And writing. And calling. And writing. I got even more scared. The settlers kept me calm. They did nothing else but keep me calm as they skimmed hundreds of dollars off my savings each month.

One day it dawned on me that the settlers weren't doing anything for me. The credit card companies were still dealing with me directly, offering me settlements, filing lawsuits against me, etc. I told the setters to take a hike. It was a great decision. If you're in a contract with a settler, write them a letter NOW and stop paying them!

When I remarried, my wife and I knew we had to get out of debt. I thank God she is very good with money and hates debt as much as I do. We're a great team. We explored all the options discussed in this book, but our combined debt and some unfortunate income reductions were too much for us. After careful and prayerful consideration, and seeking a lot of advice, we filed for Chapter 7 bankruptcy.

I hope by telling you all this you can see that I had to deal with debt on a fairly large scale, and have experienced what you're probably going through. I have lived this stuff, researched it, tried it, done it, and learned most of it the hard way. This book is my gift to you, and I hope you do better than I did, no matter what you're going through.

Types of Debt

Secured Debt is guaranteed by some form of collateral. Examples are home mortgages, auto loans or leases, alimony, and child support. The collateral for a home mortgage is obvious – your home. Alimony and child support aren't backed by collateral, per se. But since you can be held in contempt of court and even jailed for failure to pay them, they are considered secured debts. If you default on secured debts, you simply give up your collateral or go to jail. We will not be discussing secured debts at length in this book.

Unsecured Debt is the kind that you can get into without any collateral. Examples are credit cards, personal loans, and medical bills. Creditors can come after you with lawsuits to collect their money, and if they win (they usually do), then they can come after your property. The legal process, and how to deal with it, is discussed later in this book.

Good News - you can get out of debt and stay out

Getting completely out of debt is GOOD – good for your health, your marriage, and your future. And it is possible for you, just as it was for me. It's not easy, and it will take sacrifice, no matter how you do it. But the satisfaction of breaking free from debt is truly sweet.

There are many ways you can get out of debt. You can pay it off by (1) making minimum payments for fifty years, (2) consolidation, (3) roll up, (4) settlement, (5) bankruptcy, or (6) Endless Collections and Lawsuits.

Settling, lawsuits, and declaring bankruptcy damage your credit report, but you can repair your credit quickly if you know what to do. I will show you how to repair your credit.

Despite the crazy ads of the settlers (and consolidators and attorneys), you can get out of debt by yourself. It is a demanding but straightforward process. You are about to enter the secret world of the credit card companies, settlers, collection agencies, the IRS, credit reporting agencies, and the Courts. You can deal with them all if you just know what *their* tactics are and how to beat them.

Chapter 2 - The Secrets

Everyone in the credit game is after one thing – your money. The credit card companies, the collection agencies, the settlers and consolidators, the attorneys, and the IRS are all looking for ways to take money out of your pockets and put it into theirs. Let's look at some of the tricks of the trade:

Credit Card Company Secrets

Credit card companies pretty much all work the same. When you stop paying:

- Your interest rate skyrockets, and they charge you late fees, and over-limit fees if you're over your credit limit.
- If you miss another payment they put a note on your statement reminding you you're late.
- At about month 3 they start writing you letters and calling you.
- At about month 4 they start demanding you pay them and threatening to turn your account over to their legal department and/or collections. Since they're afraid you're not going to pay them, they start offering deals. For example, they might offer to stop charging fees if you start paying them again.
- At about month 5 they may hand it over to their own or an outside collection agency. About the same time they may offer you a settlement (accept part of your balance as payment in full).

- This is called "aging your accounts". The older the accounts get the better the settlement you can get from the creditor.
- The collection agency calls and writes letters and calls and writes more letters.
- If they find out you're paying another creditor or they have access to your bank account, they assume you have the money to pay them, and they may not agree to a settlement.
- They put black marks on your credit report (late payments, over limit, etc.).
- At month 6 they "charge off" your account as a bad debt and take the tax write-off.
- They report the charge off to the credit reporting agencies.
- After that, they usually sell the debt to a collection agency.
- You still owe the money even after your account has been charged off.
- After your account is charged off, it just sits. No more interest is charged in most cases and late fees stop piling up.
- Even though they have written off your debt and taken the tax break, someone will still try to collect from you.
- The amount they write-off as a bad debt, they report to the IRS as income to you, and you may have to pay taxes on that income.
- They may file a Complaint in court and ask for a default judgment against you. If they get it, you then legally owe them, and they can go after your property.
- If the Statute of Limitations for your state has passed they can't sue you (See Chapter 12 on dealing with lawsuits).
- Unless you owe child support or alimony, you can't be arrested for not paying your debts, even IRS debts (based on current laws).

Debt Settlement Company Secrets

Although the debt settlement or consolidation companies (settlers) will reveal some little known gems of truth about how the credit card companies deal with delinquent debts, there are also secrets, about themselves, the settlers don't want you to know. They will all tell you something like this:

> 'We will help you lower your monthly payments and stop the late fees, interest charges, and creditor calls. We will deal directly with the credit card companies so you don't have to. We will negotiate with them to help you settle your accounts so that you pay only a fraction of what you owe.'

YOU CAN SETTLE OR CONSOLIDATE YOUR DEBTS WITHOUT PAYING A DEBT SETTLEMENT COMPANY!

Their whole spiel is nonsense. The truth is, you're not making any payments to your creditors. You're putting money in a savings account, saving up for an amount the creditor will settle the account for. The settler takes their share from that savings account every month.

The creditor is the only entity that can decide to stop the late and over-limit fees. Nobody can stop the credit calls but you. And the only way to do it is to write the creditor a "do not call" or "cease-and-desist" letter or tell them you're declaring bankruptcy (and they will still call you until you give them an actual bankruptcy case number).

Settlers sometimes leave out the fact that some creditors will eventually file lawsuits against you to get a money judgment. The judgment allows the creditor to get a legal, binding document that says you owe them the money, and to take your wages or your property. Even though in some cases the lawsuit is filed just to scare you, many of your defaulted accounts will result in judgments against you unless you know what to do and when to do it.

The settlers are depending on your fear to keep you intimidated and needy for an advocate. What they don't explain to you is that you can settle with creditors for pennies on the dollar on your own, without any help.

- In the end, **YOU** have to do the saving and deal with creditor hassles anyway.
- The only thing the debt settler did for me was assure me I wasn't going to jail or going crazy. My Mom could have done that! The settlers essentially do nothing!
- They put **YOU** on a payment plan.
- **YOU** save a certain amount each month in a savings account.
- Each month, the settler dips into **YOUR** savings account and takes their share, usually several hundred dollars.

> *As they pamper your weary soul over the phone, they slip their hand behind your back and reach into your savings account for another draw...*

- For paying their fee, they promise to act as a buffer between you and your creditors and negotiate a settlement with the creditor when **YOU** have enough saved.
- They promise to talk to the creditors and keep them off your back (stop the calls, which they can NOT do).
- Then they tell **YOU** to call the creditors **YOURSELF** and tell them to quit calling you.
- They warn **YOU** not to tell your creditors that you are working with a debt settlement company – it lessens **YOUR** chances of getting a good settlement.
- **YOU** will still get hit with lawsuits from your creditors.
- **YOU** can negotiate your own settlements with your creditors.

Here is a screen capture of my payment plan, before I got wise to them and told them to get lost. Luckily, I didn't end up paying them the entire $6,225!:

5. **Enrolled Creditor Accounts:** The representation of the CLIENT by ~~DEBT REGRET~~ is for the resolution of outstanding debts with only the following enrolled creditors accounts and ONLY by way of negotiation and/or settlement:

Creditors
CitiFinancial Services, Inc.*
American Express - Blue
Chase
Discover Card

6. **Fee Structure:** CLIENT represents that the amount of debt entered into ~~DEBT REGRET's~~ debt settlement program is correct to the best of CLIENT'S knowledge and listed in the FEE PAYMENT SCHEDULE table below. CLIENT acknowledges and agrees with ~~DEBT REGRETS~~ estimated Time Period, Total Monthly Payment, Service Fee, and CLIENT Total Savings estimates. CLIENT understands and acknowledges that the final fee structure is determined by actual creditor statements once they are received by ~~DEBT REGRET~~. CLIENT must contact ~~DEBT REGRET~~, during normal business hours, to change payment dates. CLIENT is required to provide ~~DEBT REGRET~~ with a minimum of 5 business days to make said changes. CLIENT understands that ~~DEBT REGRET~~ is not responsible for fees or costs incurred by CLIENT associated with changes made to payment amounts or other financial decisions.

FEE PAYMENT SCHEDULE		charges a 15% Service Fee for all services provided				
Time Period	TOTAL Budget Payment	Enrollment Fee	Maintenance Fee	Additional Fee	Amount of TOTAL Budget into Client Savings (used for Settlements)
Months: 1-6	$634.03	$415.00	$0.00	$0.00	$219.03
Months: 7-18	$634.03	$311.25	$0.00	$0.00	$322.78
Months: 19-36	$634.03	$0.00	$0.00	$0.00	$634.03
Estimated Totals:	$22,825.08	$6,225	$0	$0	$16,600.08

You're not going to jail, and you won't go crazy. Hang in there.

Now – I've done everything a debt settler would do. Smile – **YOU** just saved several thousand dollars!

Collection Agency Secrets

Collection agencies are either part of the creditor's parent company or hired by the creditor to hound you until you pay them. Or, the collection agency buys your debt from the creditor for a discount and tries to collect from you.

Some are reasonable and friendly; some are downright nasty. There are rules that limit what they can do, and the rules are found in a Federal Trade Commission document called the Fair Debt Collection Practices Act (FDCPA). I recommend you visit http://www.ftc.gov/bcp/edu/pubs/consumer/credit/cre27.pdf, and read it, when you have time. To summarize it:

- They must quit calling or writing you if you write them a letter telling them you refuse to pay the debt or to stop communicating with you (known as a *cease and desist* letter).

- They cannot call you before 8:00 am or after 9:00 pm.
- They cannot call you at work if they know your employer doesn't approve.
- They cannot harass, oppress, or abuse you in any way (no threats, profanity, etc.).
- If you have an attorney, the collector can only talk to your attorney.
- They can't use false or misleading information to threaten or coerce you.
- If you inform them in writing within 30 days of their first communication, that you dispute the debt, they must verify the validity of your debt (provide you the identity of the original creditor and verification of the debt or copy of the judgment if applicable) before they can pursue it further.
- If the Statute of Limitations in your state is already passed, they can't sue you.

IRS Secrets

The IRS has considerably more power to take your money than other creditors. I don't recommend cheating on your taxes or underpaying them. The results can be very painful.

There are ways to negotiate with the IRS. The best way to learn the facts about how the IRS works is to visit their website, www.IRS.gov, and search on your topic of interest. You can find what you're looking for if you look hard enough. It's easier to talk to a tax accountant, but the IRS website is free.

The IRS is not only involved if you owe them money. They also come into play when a creditor forgives (charges off) part of your balance when you negotiate a settlement. When the creditor charges off part (or all, in some cases) of your balance, they report it to the IRS as a loss and they get a tax break. The IRS, on the other hand, adds the amount to your taxable income for that year.

A creditor files a Form 1099-C (Cancellation of Debt) when they charge off a debt greater than $600. They also send a copy of this

Form 1099-C to you. You have to file it with your income tax return and include the amount in your taxable income.

In some cases you may not owe taxes on the 1099-C amount. If you are insolvent (if your assets are less than your liabilities), you will not owe tax on your charged-off debt. In that case you would file IRS Form 982 (http://www.irs.gov/pub/irs-pdf/f982.pdf). Check with a tax accountant or research the IRS website to make sure they haven't changed the rules since you obtained this book.

> **Get professional advice when dealing with the IRS!**

You can negotiate a settlement with the IRS if you qualify. They call it an Offer In Compromise (OIC). You have probably heard or seen ads for attorneys who will handle your tax problems, right? They are talking about helping you get an Offer In Compromise. Just like you don't need a settler to get a credit card debt settlement, you don't need an attorney to get an OIC - you can do it yourself.

I recommend speaking with a good tax accountant first. They can help you decide whether to even try for an OIC, and help you make sure you're filling out the forms correctly.

To apply for an OIC, fill out Form 656 (http://www.irs.gov/pub/irs-pdf/f656.pdf). The IRS website has a pamphlet you can read about Offers In Compromise, Publication 656-B (http://www.irs.gov/pub/irs-pdf/f656b.pdf).

Here are some things to keep in mind:

- The IRS will not put you in jail.
- They will allow you to pay a bill on a payment plan (http://www.irs.gov/individuals/article/0,,id=149373,00.html). You can use Form 433D (http://www.irs.gov/pub/irs-pdf/f433d.pdf) or apply online. You must apply for a payment plan and have it approved.
- The penalties and interest on an IRS repayment plan are very high. It is recommended that you pay them off as fast

as you can, even if you have to borrow money to do it. I do not advise using credit cards!
- To qualify for an OIC, you have to demonstrate a hardship. You can use Form 656, and may have to fill out other forms. **This is not an easy task, and although you can do this yourself, a tax attorney or accountant should be consulted.**
- You can apply for Innocent Spouse Relief if you and your spouse owe a tax bill that was caused by your spouse and out of your control. You can use Form 8857 (http://www.irs.gov/pub/irs-pdf/f8857.pdf) which is explained in Publication 971 (http://www.irs.gov/pub/irs-pdf/p971.pdf).
- The IRS will take money right out of your bank account if you are in default. They call it a levy.
- The IRS doesn't care if your ex-spouse is required by law to pay a joint tax debt (i.e. in your divorce decree). If the IRS finds money in your account, and your name is on the tax return, they will take the money out of your account (levy).

Debt Collection Attorney Secrets

This is where do-it-yourself debt elimination gets tricky. Since I am not an attorney, I can't represent you, and I can't give you legal advice. All I can do is point out some facts that may surprise you and share my personal experience.

I am not against the legal profession, and I have benefitted greatly from attorneys' advice and assistance. I have trusted and dear friends who are attorneys.

On the other hand, I have learned the hard way that many of my legal battles could have been fought and won (or inevitably lost) without an attorney, and I could have kept many thousands of dollars in my pocket. I have also learned that your choice of attorney is extremely important, and that some are better than others.

If you ever find yourself in a legal situation you are unfamiliar with, or uncomfortable dealing with, I absolutely recommend hiring an attorney to advise or represent you. In some cases, their fees can be much less than a terrible outcome in court.

Ask around for referrals of a good attorney. Read reviews online. Call them and talk to them personally before you pay for a consultation, and get a consultation before you hire them for anything. The $200 - $300 for an hour's worth of advice is almost always worth it, and you can get an idea whether you like or trust them or not.

Here are a few things I've learned about attorneys and lawsuits:

- You can represent yourself in court. It's known as *pro se*, or "for yourself".
- Attorneys will give you advice, for a fee, but will rarely coach you through the *pro se* process. You're on your own. You have to educate yourself by researching your state's laws and statutes and court rules of procedure.
- Each state, and each circuit court within each state, has resources you can use to educate yourself on the local legal system. There are procedures and forms for everything, and you can find them online. Search for "[your state] statutes".
- If people knew court procedures and statutes well, most attorneys would go out of business, like doctors would if most people took good care of themselves.
- Still, there seems to be a tendency for the legal profession to "protect their own", and even if you're smarter and more prepared than an opposing attorney, you may still be defeated and embarrassed in court.
- Attorneys will most likely do as little as they can to get your case closed.
- Attorneys usually won't get emotionally involved with your dilemma, and don't care about your outcome as much as you do.
- Attorneys won't risk their reputations unless the potential rewards are huge. If you're on a tight budget, they're not going to go out on a limb for you in court. They'll take what they can get, as far as bargains and verdicts, doing what they have to do in order to stay in good graces with the judge and their fellow attorneys.

- Attorneys will charge you for EVERYTHING (phone calls, copying, electrons, toilet paper, oxygen, etc.).
- Self-representation is usually not as successful as attorney-representation, but sometimes an attorney can actually lose a case for you that you could have won yourself (it has happened to me).
- Attorneys often work within the bounds of common practice, rather than the letter of written court procedures and applicable statutes. If you know your court procedures and statutes, you can demand justice, when an attorney may let something slide because they don't want to make waves.
- When you represent yourself, you can lose by virtue of procedural tactics, even if you have a good case and justice is on your side. Attorneys know tricks and traps that can deprive you of a good outcome if you don't know what you're doing (objections, defenses, rules of procedure, legal doctrines, time limitations, etc.).
- When you're dealing with **foreclosure**, you may be risking the very roof over your head to try to fight it on your own. I **highly recommend a good attorney.**
- Answering a simple law suit for a collections complaint is fairly straightforward. You may have a good defense, especially if the Statute of Limitations has run out. On the other hand, you may be certain to lose, but if you go *pro se*, at least you saved the hundreds or thousands of dollars you would have spent on an attorney.
- There is no better feeling than winning in court, *pro se*, against an attorney because you came prepared, confident, and ready to fight.

Chapter 3 - Which Debt Elimination Strategy Should You Use?

The most morally sound, satisfying, and advantageous way to get out of debt is to simply pay it off. How you pay it off will depend on how much you can scrape together each month to either make payments or save up for settlements.

To figure out what payments you are able to make, you will have to create a budget. Creating a budget isn't as hard as it seems. Just write down all of your expenses, add them up, and compare the total to your total income. Obviously, if your expenses exceed your income, you have to make adjustments by cutting your spending or making more money.

> **How much can you pay each month?**

For guidance on creating your budget, go read the next two chapters in this book. Then come back to this chapter with an idea of how much you can afford to pay on your debts every month.

Your best plan of attack depends on how much you can afford to pay each month. We'll go through each strategy and a good process for deciding which one is best for you. The choices discussed in this book are: (1) Making Minimum Payments, (2) Consolidation, (3) Roll Up, (4) Settlement, (5) Bankruptcy, and (6) Endless Collections and Lawsuits.

Making Minimum Payments - I recommend you forget about making minimum monthly payments. How many years do you think it would take? It would have taken me almost fifty years, and I would have paid the credit card companies tens of thousands of dollars in interest. Most people will find this a solid enough motivation to eliminate their debt in some faster way.

Consolidation is taking out a loan large enough to pay off your other loans. It gives you the convenience of one monthly payment, usually quite a bit lower than the total of your previous payments. It is usually accomplished by taking out a second mortgage or home equity loan.

I do not recommend this strategy because it is too tempting to get comfortable with this new lower monthly payment, and your new loan may take you several years to pay off. Too many people just keep maxing out the equity in their home with refinancing or home equity loans. Remember, the objective is to eliminate your debt, not make it more comfortable or convenient.

If you have enough equity in your home and good enough credit to refinance or get a home equity loan, you can take this route, but you most likely won't be getting out of debt for a long, long, time. It is also a risky move since the value of your home may decrease, leaving you in a situation where you owe more than your home is worth – your collateral goes away, and you have another, possibly very large, unsecured debt to deal with – the kind that can result in the nightmare of foreclosure.

Roll up (sometimes known as "snowball") is where you make extra payments on your lowest balance account while making minimum payments on all other accounts. You don't worry about interest rates – the roll up system works and has the psychological advantage of creating momentum

> *If you can pay 20% or more above your total monthly minimum payments, Roll Up is a great strategy*

as you hammer one account after another. Once you pay your lowest balance off, you start on your next lowest balance, and so on.

Roll up is an excellent choice if you have the cash flow to do it. If you are serious about getting out of debt (and I know you are), you should maximize your cash flow and use whatever means you have to attack that first account. As you gain momentum and confidence, you apply the same principles as you pay off the rest of your accounts.

Sell your surfboard. Buy an older car for cash and eliminate a car payment. Downsize your house. Follow a budget. Live within your means. Slaughter your debt!

If you can free up 20% or more above your total monthly minimum payments, debt roll up is an excellent strategy. You will not only preserve your credit score, but you will most likely improve it. And you will have the satisfaction of having paid your debts off in full.

Let's say you have $37,000 in total unsecured debts, and all your monthly minimum payments add up to $370. Add 20% to $370 as follows:

$$\$370 \times 1.2 = \$444$$

If you can manage to pay $444 each month, then debt roll up will work for you.

Settlement is where the creditor agrees to accept a fraction of your balance as payment in full.

In forgiving part of your debt, they get a tax break by writing it off as a bad debt. They call it "charging off" your account.

When your account "ages", the creditor starts to worry about your ability or willingness to pay. At a certain point they decide it's better to get something from you than nothing, especially if they suspect you might be contemplating bankruptcy. They start negotiating by offering to stop the late and over-limit fees, reverse some of the interest charges, etc., in order to get you to pay something.

At about the 5 month point, they start to soften up to the idea of an offer. Sometimes they make an offer to you. If so, you counter their offer with a lesser amount. People have been known to settle for as little as 20% of the balance.

You can make offers to the creditor around month four or five, and by then, they are ready to work with you. You can write them a letter to offer a settlement, but calling them can get faster results. Just be ready to negotiate on the phone, and if you do reach an agreement, get it in writing before you pay anything.

If you meet the following criteria, settlement is probably your best option:

- You can stomach the temporary obliteration of your credit report and score.
- You are prepared to live on a budget, within your means, debt free.
- You don't have the cash flow to pay your accounts off by roll up or feel it would take you too long.
- You are willing to stop all payments to all unsecured creditors.
- You can manage to monthly put away around 2% or more of your total combined unsecured debt to save up for settlements.

Settlement is easy, but painful. To succeed at debt settlement, you need:

a. Patience
b. Discipline
c. A good reason to ruin your credit score (like the genuine inability to pay)
d. knowledge of how to do it
e. A support system to tell you they still love you once in a while

Although the settlement process is hard on your credit report, it is a proven way to eliminate your credit card debt, and if you meet strict qualification requirements, your IRS debt too. You can also negotiate settlements for other kinds of unsecured debt, like medical bills, personal loans, student loans, etc. In some cases, you can even obtain a settlement on a second mortgage or a home equity line of credit (HELOC) – see Chapter 8. Your credit report can be repaired significantly within a few months.

If you can save at least 2% of your total unsecured debt balance each month, settlement is a good option. Let's say your total unsecured debt is $37,000. 2% is calculated as follows:

$$37,000 \times 0.02 = 740$$

If you can put away 2% each month to save for settlements, you should be able to do just fine. The more you can save each month, the faster you can be done with the whole process.

Bankruptcy is the legal process that requires creditors to totally forgive your debts (Chapter 7) or let you pay them off, either partially or in full, on a payment plan (Chapter 13). To determine your eligibility for either Chapter, you must complete a Means Test, which determines how much you have left over every month after expenses.

You must also prove to the Court that your debts did not come about by fraud (spending gobs of money on credit while intending to declare bankruptcy).

A Trustee (like a court-appointed lawyer) is assigned to your case to review it for accuracy and make sure you're not hiding assets or committing fraud, and liquidate (sell) your unnecessary assets. You get to keep basic necessities and you are allowed to keep secured debts intact (like car loans and mortgages) if you choose, but you have to keep making payments to keep the property. The rest of your *unnecessary* belongings are sold at auction and the proceeds are used to pay creditors. The Trustee decides which belongings are considered *unnecessary*.

If you are caught hiding assets, you can be charged with fraud and go to jail. I declared Chapter 7 bankruptcy. I did not have to give up any property for liquidation. The Trustee was fair and reasonable and helped me through the process.

If you don't meet the eligibility requirements for Chapter 7 or just prefer to repay some of your debts, Chapter 13 establishes a repayment plan. If you successfully complete the repayment plan, all the rest of your unsecured debts are forgiven. The repayment plan takes into consideration how much you can afford to pay, both in monthly payments, and total amount.

The Means Test is like a giant loan application where you list all your income, assets, debts, and monthly expenses. Depending on your gross monthly income, how much money you're left with at the end of the month, whether you're married, and how many children you have, you may or may not qualify to declare bankruptcy at all. If you're even thinking about declaring bankruptcy, you should fill out a Means Test to see which Chapter, if either, you qualify for. You should also read an excellent overview called Bankruptcy Basics (written by the Federal Bankruptcy Court) by visiting: http://www.uscourts.gov/FederalCourts/Bankruptcy/BankruptcyBasics.aspx.

The Means Test is elaborate, and ignorance is not acceptable in Bankruptcy Court as an excuse for mistakes. I highly recommend a consultation with a tax accountant or attorney once you have done your best at filling out the Means Test. If you are considering bankruptcy for your business, the rules are different than for individuals, and you would be ill advised to do it without professional assistance.

You can find the means testing Form B22A online by visiting: http://www.uscourts.gov/uscourts/RulesAndPolicies/rules/BK_Forms_Official_2010/B_022A_0410.pdf. You have to go to a few different websites and figure out what your state and county's allowances are for food, transportation, etc., as part of the calculation. Don't worry, it isn't that complicated. Just follow the process.

Bankruptcy is much worse, in many ways, than settlement. It stays on your credit report for up to 10 years. You have no choice but to live within your means (not a bad thing) because you are not allowed to declare bankruptcy again for at least 7 years, and it is very hard to obtain any kind of credit for a while afterwards. Unless you have VA loan eligibility and your reason for declaring bankruptcy was out of your control, you can't even be considered for a mortgage for two years.

The good news is, there are ways, discussed later in this book, to rebuild your credit score in as little as one year after bankruptcy. And if you are eligible for a VA loan, your credit report since bankruptcy is spotless, you have rebuilt your credit score, you have been paying rent or a mortgage, and your reason for declaring bankruptcy was out of your control, you may be able to get a mortgage after one year.

If you meet the following criteria, you may want to seriously consider declaring bankruptcy:

- You cannot pay about 20% above your total monthly minimum payments each month.
- You cannot save 2% or more of your total unsecured debt each month for settlements.
- You are prepared to live on a budget, within your means, debt free.
- You are not able or willing to make minimum payments for the next several decades in order to pay off your unsecured debts.
- You have not placed yourself at risk for being charged with fraud.

Endless Collections and Lawsuits

 - sounds nice, doesn't it? This is the method by which you forfeit your chances of ever obtaining a mortgage, and quite possibly, a job. Have you ever applied for a job or a loan where the application asked if you have ever had a judgment against you? Mortgage applications certainly include this question.

If you default on your debt obligations and don't proactively eliminate your debt, the creditors will have no trouble obtaining judgments against you in court. A judgment is a legal, binding document that gives the creditor legal rights to collect what you owe. If you don't have money, they can confiscate your property and sell it to get their money.

You don't want creditors calling you day after day. You don't want to wake up in the morning and find your car missing. You want to pay off your debts, one way or another. If you absolutely can't pay them, you need to bite the bullet and get free by declaring bankruptcy. As I can testify, there is life after bankruptcy.

Debt Elimination Strategy Decision Tool

In summary, let's review and make a decision. Answer the following questions and decide on your debt elimination strategy:

1. Am I ready to get out of debt? _____

2. Am I going to develop a budget? _____

3. How much do I owe in unsecured debt (total debt)? _____

4. How much can I free up each month for payments? _____

5. Can I pay at least 20% above my total min. pmts. each month? _____
   DEBT ROLL UP IS MY STRATEGY (skip the rest of the questions and study Chapter 7)

6. Can I save at least 2% of my total debt each month for settlements, and I am prepared for a dip in my credit score? _____
   SETTLEMENT IS MY STRATEGY (skip the rest of the questions and study Chapter 8)

7. Can I not free up enough to Roll Up or Settle my debt? _____
   BANKRUPTCY IS MY STRATEGY
   (study Chapter 9)

Chapter 4 - The Almighty Budget

If you learn and apply anything from this book, let it be budgeting. If you do, you will easily save yourself, in a few months or years, a thousand times the price you paid for these words. Getting out of debt is only a pipe dream without a budget. If you are going to get out of debt, and hopefully, stay out, your budget is the first step, and one you can't skip. You can't even make an informed decision on which strategy to use to get out of debt until you have made a simple budget.

Before we discuss how to budget, let's be clear on why to budget. As I said at the beginning of this book, strife caused by debt and financial issues is arguably the number one reason for divorce. Debt and divorce are kissing cousins – debt is both the top cause of, and a common result from, divorce. And the number one cause of debt (actually the ONLY cause of debt)? **Overspending.**

Spending more than you make is what creates debt in the first place. And why do people spend more than they make? Two reasons:

- They don't keep track of what they spend (they don't have a budget)
- They don't care if they overspend (whether they have a budget or not)

Budgeting isn't easy if you're used to spending more than you make or you generally ignore your finances. I used to control my finances like an amoeba – changing shape every Christmas, every vacation, every time I decided I needed something right now, whenever I felt like having a candy bar, etc.

Budgeting is also not easy if you and your spouse don't talk openly about money. Do you know what your spouse is spending? Does he know what you're spending? Are you afraid to tell each other? What's there to lose? Your marriage? Your retirement?

I don't mean to be a downer, but this is serious business. Financial matters are at the heart of almost every aspect of life. And your budget is the heart of your financial matters. Businesses and nations live or die by their budgets. So do marriages, families, relationships, and retirements.

Let's go a little off-topic, for married people or those thinking about getting married, and talk about your marriage. Budgeting is a sensitive issue. If you're having trouble dealing with this and other sensitive issues, maybe you could use a marriage tune-up or even a marriage rescue. From experience, I would recommend two resources to anyone married or even thinking about getting married. One is The Love Dare. It is a book and devotional you can buy in paper form or as an App for your smart phone.

Another excellent resource for anyone wanting to save or improve their marriage is the Marriage Fitness system by Mort Fertel. I recommend you sign up for his free email series called "7 Secrets for Fixing Your Marriage", even if your marriage doesn't need fixing! It's bound to help you in your quest for better communication and building the connection you either lost or never had with your spouse, or enhancing what you already have. You can check it out by visiting http://www.mortfertel.com/cmd.asp?af=1273728.

Budgeting is simply knowing and planning what you spend. You add up what you bring in each month, compare it to what you spend each month, and decide where to adjust in order to reach your goals.

If your goal is to retire by age 45, you have to have a plan. If your goal is to pay for your children's college, again, you'd better have a plan. If you would like to buy your wife that massive rock you couldn't afford when you got married, get to work on your budget!

A "balanced budget" is where you spend as much as you make. A step above the balanced budget is where you are saving money each month. Another step above that is where you are saving *and giving* money to charity each month.

Discretionary spending includes anything you don't need to survive or do your job. The things you need to survive and do your job are your house, food, clothing, car, and things like taxes, insurance, phone, etc. Some things that are considered necessities cross over into discretionary spending, like:

- Designer clothes
- Fancy cars
- Lavish homes
- Gourmet food
- Cadillac phone plans

You may need to cut discretionary spending to balance your budget. Or you may need to make cuts in order to get quickly out of debt, or to increase savings or charitable giving. Whatever your reasons are, cutting discretionary spending will help your financial situation.

If every bit of discretionary spending is trimmed out of your budget, and you still can't balance it, you either have to increase your income, or stop making some of your payments. You can turn a leased car back in and either buy a cheap car or do without. You can negotiate payment holidays (skipped payments) with your mortgage banker or credit card companies. In some cases, if you have lost your job or part of your income, stopping payments may be unavoidable.

Ultimately, if you cannot make all your payments, you will have to decide which ones to stop paying. Even though it may be tempting to stop making mortgage payments because they are relatively large, keep in mind that foreclosure is much more damaging to your credit score and future borrowing ability than defaulting on a credit card, and losing your home is worse than losing your good credit score.

While negotiating a loan modification or repayment plan with your mortgage lender is possible, and simply involves calling your lender, discussing your options, and following their directions, this book focuses on dealing with credit cards and other unsecured debts.

Saving an Emergency Fund

Many financial teachers recommend saving an emergency fund. I agree wholeheartedly, and recommend you do it in two steps. First, save $1,000 as fast as you can. Sell some stuff. Give up lattes or golf for a month, whatever it takes. That $1,000 may come in handy. You know as well as I do that unexpected things happen, and your mini-fund will help you not have to fall back into the credit card trap.

The second step is to save up about three months of your take home pay. I recommend setting a minimum target of $10,000. This should cover more serious emergencies. Remember, this is an *emergency* fund, not a vacation or Christmas fund.

Are you ready to slay your debt? Ok, **finally**, let's get to the how-to!

Chapter 5 - How to Create a Budget

Use the checklist in Chapter 16 to keep you organized and track your progress.

To create your budget, add up your monthly incomes and subtract your monthly expenses. You can create a simple excel spreadsheet or scribble it down on a napkin, as long as you cover all your ins and outs. There is a picture and an explanation of the excel spreadsheet that I use at the end of this chapter.

Step One – Discuss budgeting with your spouse and family, or anyone you are involved with financially.

Step Two - Start saving receipts for budget design/review (if you use cash).

Step Three – Set goals.

Don't worry about timing right now. Just dream of where you want to be – debt free? millionaire? financially independent? Giving 20% to charity? Riding the "balanced" line and getting by each month? Write it down.

Step Four – Add up all your monthly gross incomes.

Start by totaling all your income streams. How much gross pay do you and/or your spouse or other household contributors receive each month? How about Social Security benefits? VA benefits? Child support? Alimony? Interest income that you actually use as income and don't reinvest? Any other sources of monthly income?

Step Five – Add up all monthly expenses.

The harder part is expenses. You would be surprised at what you're spending when you shine a flashlight on it. And it may be more difficult to figure out if you use credit cards, debit cards, *and* cash!

If you only use credit and/or debit cards, you can review your monthly card and bank statements to figure out how much you're spending on different things.

If you use cash, you can look at your receipts, if you've kept them. It's a good idea to keep all your receipts for a couple of months in order to better understand what you're spending money on. It's also a great idea because it allows you to verify whether or not you're following your budget.

Count your auto-deductions from your paychecks as expenses. You can find your monthly tax and insurance expenses by reviewing your pay statement if you get one. You may have automatic withdrawals that go to your 401K. Count them as expenses.

Step Six – Subtract monthly expenses from monthly income.

Step Seven - If your budget doesn't show a monthly excess, cut spending to bring your budget into balance.

Once you have a pretty good idea of what you have been spending, and your monthly excess or shortfall, it's time to make some decisions about how you're spending your money.

Step Eight - Brainstorm ways to free up more money for debt elimination (or savings, retirement, giving, etc.).

Can you sell some things? Can you work a second job? Can you start a small business selling goods, services, or ideas? Can you cut down your dining out each month? Do you need premium cable channels? Do you need a land-line or can you get by with only your cell phone? Do you need to buy Cheerios or can you get by with generic Pookie O's? Can you cut your own lawn? Can you train your children to cut your own lawn?

Step Nine – Plan how much you will spend on discretionary items (dining out, vacations, Christmas gifts, etc.)

Step Ten - Brainstorm ways to make more money.

Get out a blank sheet of paper and brainstorm on how you can save or make more money. Write down as many things you can think of. Don't worry about whether they're realistic or sensible. Just dump your ideas on paper. Then walk away for a while, come back, and add some more. Walk away again, then sit down and look your list over and pick a few you can do right now. It's a great way to tighten up your budget and free up more ammo for your fight to eradicate debt from your life.

Step Eleven - Set goals for how to spend, save, and give money in the future.

Step Twelve - Discuss your budget with family members and get buy-in.

Step Thirteen - Create enthusiasm for debt elimination and saving.

Step Fourteen - Consider using only cash to curb impulsive use of plastic .

- Save receipts!!!

Step Fifteen - Track your budget by tracking all spending.

Step Sixteen - Adjust budget as you learn or circumstances change.

Step Seventeen (recommended) - Read "The Total Money Makeover". You will appreciate the personal stories and get some good motivation to live on a budget and get debt free.

Step Eighteen (recommended) - Read "Rich Dad, Poor Dad". You will benefit from a brand new perspective on money – your money, your children's money, and your grand-children's money.

Step Nineteen (recommended) - Read "The Richest Man in Babylon". This is one of the most fascinating books on money I have ever read.

Step Twenty (recommended) – Read "The Greatest Salesman in the World", another mind-blowing book on money, character, and attitude. This is a must-read. Ask your spouse to read it. Ask your high school kid to write a one page book report on it.

Step Twenty One – Study personal finance. This should be a part of everyone's personal journey. Money is very important, and how you make it, how you spend it, what priority you give it, whether you save it or spend it all, whether you are generous with it, are all part of your very identity. If you're interested, do word searches in the

Bible on "money", "giving", "the rich", "the poor", "lender", "borrower", etc. The Bible has a LOT to say about money.

A picture of the budget I've used for several years is shown below. It is in Microsoft Excel, and it is very simple. You don't need to use Excel or any spreadsheet for that matter. You could use a notebook with a table on it made with a pencil and a ruler. Just make one!

In my budget spreadsheet, I have lumped things together into groups. You may want to arrange things differently. I simply summed the columns of expenses, summed all incomes, and subtracted expenses from income.

I like to gage my progress toward my financial goals by figuring out my spending and saving percentages too. You can sum certain groups (like charitable giving) and divide that number by your total gross income to get the percentage. To see your savings percentage, sum all savings and divide by total gross income. You get the idea. You can figure out what percentage of your income goes to taxes, insurance, food, clothing, mortgage, etc.

You can request a copy of my excel budget spreadsheet by emailing me at debtrel8@debt-relief-truth.com. You can also use a software program like Quicken or Microsoft Money, or a free budgeting tool like Mint, SimpleD, AceMoney Lite, PearBudget, etc.

Example Budget Spreadsheet

	A	B	C	D	E	F	G	H	I	J	K	L
1					It's My Money Monthly Budget							
2	Expense Description	This Month	YTD	Budgeted Amount	Expense Description	This Month	YTD	Budgeted Amount	Income Description	This Month	YTD	Planned Amount
3	Car Maintenance			40.00	Groceries			850.00	FPL			5,500.00
4	Cat Tax				Vitamins/Supplements			50.00	VA			628.00
5	Car Payment			287.00	Dining Out			150.00	Child Support			900.00
6	Car Lease Payment			279.00					Total Income	0.00		7,328.00
7	Car Insurance			650.00	Continuing ed/business/legal			25.00	Minus tax- Fed-Medic-SSC			6,781.00
8	Fuel - cars			600.00	Entertainment			30.00	Living (X)			
9					Furniture/decor			25.00	Giving (X)			
10	Boat Payment				Gym Memberships			50.00	Debt (X)			
11	Boat Maintenance				Fishing permits/supplies			10.00	Savings (X)			
12	Boat Storage							45.00	Total Expenses			7,676.43
13	Boat Insurance				Baby/young/Camp			0.00	DIFFERENCE	0.00		-338.43
14	Boat/Towing Insurance				Our children/ Birthdays			75.00				
15					Spouse - Birthday, V-day, etc.			50.00	Debts	Balance		Payment
16	Rent/Mortgage				Fam. B'day mom's day, etc.			25.00	IRS	8,000.00		105.00
17	Home Insurance				Christmas Gifts			100.00	Almonds $20k orig	5,500.00		500.00
18	Property Tax				Msn. Gifts (time/spt, etc)			400.00	Amex Blue	20,000.00		500.00
19	Lawn								Chase Visa	11,562.15		
20	Electric/Gas utilities			232.00	United Way				Discover	16,252.12		
21	Water/Sewer Utilities			50.00	Missions				Citibank MasterCard	10,132.96		
22	Home maintenance/imp				Compassion, tv evan/local				401K Loan	22,801.78		
23					Orphan's Tear				Citibank MasterCard	1,000.00		50.25
24	Life Ins (spouse)				Heaven's Family Manual Fund			120.00	Home Owners Assn	5,009.72		
25	Life Ins (children)			5.00	Church			862.00	Burdens McCool Law Firm	1,890.00		
26	Life Insurance (self)			58.48	Jowee Meyers				Doyeny Tax	5,502.72		
27	Medical/Dental Premiums			207.00	Almonds			500.00	PA	3,833.04		
28	Flex Spending Account			84.00	Dedtson			500.00	Chase Visa	3,995.25		
29	Other medical (copays, etc)			40.00	401K Loan			50.35	Macy's	18,481.43		
30					Child Support			1,000.00	American Express	190.00		
31	Give-to pop, step, apr, ad			10.00					Gamboree Visa	14,651.42		
32	Financial Planning								Chicorp	643.67		
33	Internet Service				Fed Income Tax			289.00	Toyota (car lease)	4,045.69		274.94
34	Cell Phone				SSC Tax			189.00	Wells Fargo (mortgage)	21,000.00		
35	Cable TV				Medicare Tax			59.00	GE Care One®	400,000.00		
36				25.00						4,900.00		
37	Clothes/Shoes (self)			25.00	401K (7% of salary)			350.00	Totals	586,325.70		1,655.25
38	Clothes/Shoes (children)			100.00	Savings				NOTES:			
39	Clothes/Shoes (spouse)			100.00	Kids' college							
40									Some items related to biweekly pay system were calculated per paycheck.			
41	Subtotals	0.00	0.00	2,258.00		0.00	0.00	5,189.35	x2/m2. Income is listed per pay period - two months/year an extra check is			
42	My Goals: 15% savings, 0% debt, 70% living & 15% giving											

Formula annotations:
- =SUM(L3:L5)
- =SUM(D42,H42)
- =L6-L12
- =SUM(H3:H41)
- =SUM(D3:D41)

31

Chapter 6 - How to Cut Up Your Credit Cards

TOOLS REQUIRED
- Scissors
- Leather gloves
- Impact resistant safety glasses
- Party hats, camera
- Refreshments and fancy glasses to toast

Caution

Do not insert fingers between scissor blades

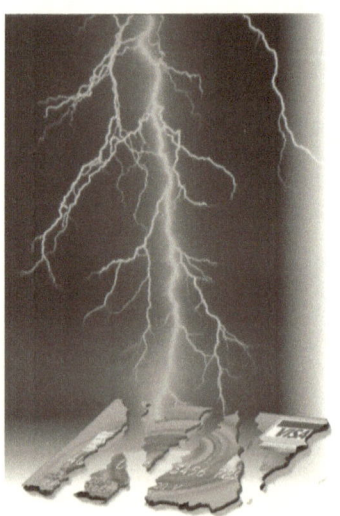

Step One – GATHER credit cards.
Step Two – CUT cards into several pieces.
    a. **ENSURE** card number and magnetic strip are segmented so as to prevent possibility of future reassembly and use by criminals.
Step Three - TAKE pictures to pass on to your children and grandchildren.
Step Four - DISPOSE of card pieces properly.
Step Five - RAISE a toast to your financial freedom.

Chapter 7 - How to Eliminate Debt by Roll Up

Your Check List is waiting for you in Chapter 16…

Roll up is where you make extra payments on your lowest balance account while making minimum payments on all other accounts. You don't worry about interest rates – the roll up system works and has the psychological advantage of creating momentum as you hammer one account after another. Once you pay your lowest balance off, you start on your next lowest balance, and so on.

Friendly reminder – debt consolidation loans are not recommended. If you want to do it, there are countless lenders who would be happy to keep you in bondage to debt and make your life more fun for a while.

Debt Roll Up is, in my opinion, the best way to go if you have the money to do it. Don't give up on it too soon – you may be able to *find* the money to do it.

Step One – Decide to Get Out of Debt And Stay Out.

Step Two – Cut Up Credit Cards (can keep 1 or 2 to maintain credit score, but pay them off completely each month).

Step Three – Design Monthly Budget.

Step Four – Save $1000 Emergency Fund.

Step Five - Sell Unneeded Belongings.

Step Six – Reduce Spending On Unneeded Items/Activities.

Step Seven – Downsize (House, Cars, etc.).

Step Eight – Make Extra Pmts on Lowest Balance Card/Loan Until Paid Off.

Don't worry about starting on the balance with the highest interest rate. Just slam the lowest balance and build momentum.

Step Nine – Make Minimum Pmts On All Other Cards/Loans Until 1st Paid Off.

Step Ten – Make Extra Pmts on 2nd Highest Balance Card/Loan Until Paid Off.

Step Eleven – Make Extra Pmts on 3rd Highest Balance Until Paid Off.

Step Twelve - Make Extra Pmts on 4th Highest Balance Until Paid Off.

Step Thirteen – Make Extra Pmts on 5th Highest Balance Until Paid Off.

Step Fourteen – Make Extra Pmts on 6th Highest Balance Until Paid Off.

Step Fifteen – Make Extra Pmts on 7th Highest Balance Until Paid Off.

Step Sixteen – Make Extra Pmts on 8th Highest Balance Until Paid Off.

Step Seventeen – Follow Cascading Payoff Until All Cards/Loans Paid Off.

Step Eighteen – File All Statements/Correspondence.

Step Nineteen – Monitor Credit Report.

Step Twenty – Save For Major Contingency Fund (Target $10,000+).

Step Twenty One – Pay Off Cars as soon as possible (ASAP).

Step Twenty Two - Pay Off Student Loans ASAP.

Step Twenty Three – Pay Off Home Equity Loans ASAP.

Step Twenty Four – Pay Off Mortgage ASAP.

Step Twenty Five – Borrow To Pay For Things That **APPRECIATE** In Value **ONLY** (like a home, but be careful – homes don't *always* go up in value).

Chapter 8 - How to Eliminate Debt by Settlement

Use the check list from Chapter 16.
Follow the timeline in the check list as closely as possible.

There following are strategies that you MUST follow faithfully to succeed at settling your debts. This is an easy thing to do, but you have to do it right.

DO NOT take out large cash advances or make a bunch of purchases right before you stop making payments. The creditor may be more aggressive in suing you because it appears you are committing fraud. If you have taken out such an advance or made a recent flurry of purchases, make a few months more payments, if you can, before you start this process.

You **MUST** stop **ALL** payments. If one creditor finds out you are still paying another creditor, they will assume you have the money to pay them too, and your chances of negotiating a settlement are diminished.

You **MUST KEEP SAVING** as much as you can for settlements. If you have several accounts or large amounts to settle, you will want to save quickly so that you can pay them off by settlement preferably before the creditors start fling lawsuits.

You **MUST BE PATIENT** and let the process take its course. Remember, the more "aged" your account is, the better the settlement you can negotiate.

You **MUST MOVE YOUR MONEY** from any account associated with a creditor (e.g. Chase bank checking/savings accounts and Chase Visa credit card) to an unassociated account. The Right of Offset Law allows a creditor to take the money you refuse to pay them, from your associated checking, savings, or investment accounts, to pay your delinquent balances.

You **MUST KEEP RECORDS** of all statements, correspondence, and phone conversations. Take notes after every phone conversation, and file them away with your records.

You **MUST INSIST** on all agreements **IN WRITING**. A creditor may agree to something on the phone and conveniently "forget" later. **INSIST** on the creditor including "Paid In Full" or "Settled In Full" on their settlement agreement letter, **AND** on your Credit Report.

You **MUST** mail settlement payments **ON TIME**, and pay by **CASHIER'S CHECK** or **MONEY ORDER**, and by **REGISTERED MAIL, RETURN RECEIPT REQUESTED**.

DO NOT send a check or they will then have your bank account information.

You don't have to answer every call, but you **MUST COMMUNICATE** with the creditors, and let them know you're in a bind and can't pay them. The best way to cool them off, and also soften them up to a better settlement, is by telling them you're leaning toward declaring bankruptcy. They won't quit calling you until you provide them with an actual bankruptcy case number, so if you're bluffing, expect them to keep calling you.

You may want to find the sweet spot between settlement and getting sued with a lawsuit. I am not recommending waiting until a creditor files a lawsuit against you, but you want to keep in communication with them enough to figure out if and when they plan to sue you.

They may threaten to turn your account over to their legal department. Don't panic if they do. In fact, the FDCPA prohibits creditors from threatening you with legal action. Just keep in touch with them and if they do turn your account over to their legal department, then talk to their legal department. When they start talking about filing a lawsuit against you, it's time to get serious about making a settlement offer.

Again, you don't have to wait until they threaten a lawsuit. At the six month point, they should be softening up to a settlement offer.

Settling a second mortgage (or home equity line of credit - HELOC) can be done if you get an appraisal of your home that shows it is worth less than the first and second mortgages (or HELOC) together and you are in default for the first mortgage. Your chances are even better if your home isn't even worth the amount of the first mortgage amount. To request a settlement, mail or fax the second mortgage or HELOC holder a copy of the appraisal and proof that the first mortgage is in default.

You can also settle with your college bursar's office to pay off student loans. You need to tell them about your financial hardship. You don't need to skip payments and wait a while like you do with credit cards. You may not get as good a deal as with your other creditors, but in most cases you can negotiate a settlement and get a break.

I have included a sample settlement offer letter from a credit card company, and example offer and offer acceptance letters at the end of this chapter. Please feel free to copy the letter format and just plug in your name and your creditor's name.

Here is the step-by-step procedure for negotiating settlements with your creditors:

Step One – Decide to Get Out of Debt And Stay Out.
Step Two – Cut Up Credit Cards.
Step Three – Stop Making **ALL** Credit Card Payments.
Step Four – Design Monthly Budget.
Step Five – Open New Savings Account (unrelated to card companies).
Step Six – Start Saving At Least 2% Of Total Card Debt In New Account.
Step Seven – Sell Unneeded Belongings.
Step Eight – Reduce Spending On Unneeded Items/Activities.
Step Nine – Change Phone Number (optional).
Step Ten – Save $1000 Emergency Fund (keep in safe, confidential place)
Step Eleven - If Contacted by a Collector, Call Original Creditor to Verify Collector's Right to Collect From You and that they agree to

the settlement terms offered by the collector. The collector may have learned of your defaulted account and pursued you independently of the original creditor. If you pay the collection agency, the original creditor may still expect you to pay them too. **Note** – This is one good reason to insist on debt validation by a collection agency (See Step Thirteen. You have a right to demand validation of the debt they're trying to collect.).

Step Twelve – Mail Cease And Desist Letters To Collection Agencies (as necessary).

Step Thirteen – Insist On Validation of Debt By Collection Agencies (as necessary) Please find the example Debt Validation Letter at the end of Chapter 11.

Step Fourteen – If threatened or served with a lawsuit, Contact an Attorney For Guidance. **Note** - Although you can answer a lawsuit without an attorney it is always a good idea to consult with a qualified attorney. Again, nothing in this book is meant to be viewed as legal advice. There are also many local resources for *pro se,* or self-represented, litigants. Check your County Court website for instructions, forms, and procedures, and read Chapter 12 of this book.

Step Fifteen – File All Statements/Correspondence.

Step Sixteen - Inform Creditors of Inability to Pay.

Step Seventeen – Monitor Credit Report Monthly.

Step Eighteen – Inform Creditors of Potential Bankruptcy.

Step Nineteen – Save 25% of Largest Credit Card Balance (Creditor 1).

Step Twenty – Make Settlement Offer (or counteroffer) To Creditor 1 (see example letter at the end of this Chapter).

Step Twenty One – Insist on Written Terms of Settlement, in proper format. The following items must be on the creditor's settlement offer letter:

- Official agency letterhead with correct creditor name (e.g. Bank of America instead of FIA Card Services, or both clearly stated)
- Letter is dated
- Original account number listed correctly

- Full balance listed correctly
- Settlement amount listed correctly
- Payment due date listed correctly
- Payment instructions listed correctly
- Includes Release of Liability Clause
- Signed by a company representative

If the creditor's settlement offer letter does not contain all of the above, write or call them back and insist they send you a new one with all the required information.

Step Twenty Two – Insist on "Paid In Full" or "Settled In Full" posting to Credit Report, **AND** removal of late payments and charge-offs from credit report.

Step Twenty Three - Mail Settlement Payments by Registered Mail, Return Receipt Requested, with a copy of the creditor's settlement agreement letter.

Step Twenty Four – Mail Settlement Payments **ON TIME**.

Step Twenty Five – Pay By Cashier's Check or Money Order From Non-affiliated Bank. Take cash to a bank that you don't have an account with and ask to buy a Cashier's Check or Money Order. If you buy the Cashier's Check at your home bank, the creditor can get your account information from the Cashier's Check. You will need a few extra dollars – the bank will charge you a small fee for the transaction.

Step Twenty Six - Request settled-in-full or zero balance confirmation letter about one week after making your payment.

Step Twenty Seven – When Creditor 1 Account is Settled, Repeat Process for Creditor 2, and so on.

Step Twenty Eight – Repeat Process Until All Accounts Are Settled.

Step Twenty Nine – Answer Lawsuits As Necessary.

Note (1) - When you are served with a lawsuit, you have 20 days to file an Answer with the court. If you do not file an Answer within 20 days, the Plaintiff (creditor) can ask for a Default Judgment. A Default Judgment means you are now legally required to pay the debt, the creditor can obtain liens on your property, and the judgment hurts your credit report. It is best, even if the creditor is likely to win the lawsuit, to file your Answer before the deadline. It at least buys time to settle with the creditor and avoid the judgment. For an example of a generic Answer and a brief explanation of the process, read Chapter 12 of this book. As always, it is advisable to seek the advice of a qualified attorney.

Note (2) – Even if the creditor obtains a judgment, you may still be able to settle the debt with them.

Step Thirty – Declare Bankruptcy **ONLY IF NECESSARY.**

Step Thirty One – Repair Credit Report.

Step Thirty Two – Rebuild Credit.

Step Thirty Three – Downsize (House, Cars, etc.).

Step Thirty Four – Save For Major Contingency Fund (Target $10,000+).

Step Thirty Five – Pay Off Cars ASAP.

Step Thirty Six – Pay Off Student Loans ASAP.

Step Thirty Seven – Pay Off Home Equity Loans ASAP.

Step Thirty Eight - Pay Off Mortgage ASAP.

Step Thirty Nine- Borrow To Pay For Things That **APPRECIATE** In Value **ONLY.**

See below for examples of settlement offer letters from creditors and borrowers, and settlement agreement letters.

Example Settlement Offer From Creditor

Law Offices of
ZAKHEIM & ASSOCIATES
A PROFESSIONAL ASSOCIATION
1045 SOUTH UNIVERSITY DRIVE
SUITE 202
PLANTATION, FL 33324

SCOTT C. ZAKHEIM*
*ALSO MEMBER OF N.Y. BAR
FLYNN LA VRAR
RICHARD BATTAGLINO
SASHA HARO
SABINE MICHEL

TELEPHONE: (954) 735-4455
FAX: (954) 735-0227
WWW.ZAKHEIMLAW.COM

April 14, 2009

RE: CITIBANK (SOUTH DAKOTA), N.A. /
Account Number:
Our File Number:
Current Balance: 4,381.60   Proposed Settlement Amount: $2190.80

Dear ███████:

    CITIBANK (SOUTH DAKOTA), N.A. has instructed this office to extend to you an opportunity to fully satisfy the amount owed on the credit account referenced above. CITIBANK (SOUTH DAKOTA), N.A. will accept **$2190.80, 50% of the current balance owed,** as complete settlement of your account. To take advantage of this settlement offer your payment should be made payable to CITIBANK (SOUTH DAKOTA), N.A. and should be **received in our office by Thursday, April 30, 2009.** We accept online payments at our website www.zakheimlaw.com.

    Once your settlement payment has cleared our trust account our office will notify our client that the account has been settled and, if a judgment has been entered, a satisfaction of judgment will be prepared and recorded in the public records. Once this account is settled all collection activity will forever cease on the account. Until the account is settled however, collection activity may continue on the account.

    Should you have questions or concerns regarding this offer contact us at 800-531-5490.

Sincerely,

Zakheim & Associates, P.A.

THIS IS AN ATTEMPT TO COLLECT A DEBT AND ANY INFORMATION OBTAINED WILL BE USED FOR THAT PURPOSE. THIS COMMUNICATION IS FROM A DEBT COLLECTOR.

Zakheim & Associates
1045 S University Dr, Ste 202
Plantation, FL 33324-3333   008799

RETURN SERVICE REQUESTED

☐ My settlement payment of $2190.80 for CITIBANK (SOUTH DAKOTA), N.A. is included.

☐ I am unable to settle this account at this time. Please call me at phone number _____ to discuss other payment alternatives.

Zakheim & Associates
1045 S University Dr Ste 202
Plantation FL 33324-3333

18289**AUTO**SCH 3-DIGIT 334
                                    35
Lake Worth FL 33467-8713

Example Letter for Settlement Offer

[Date]

[Your Name]
[Your Address]
[City, State, Zip]
Fax [xxx-xxx-xxxx]

[Collector's Name]
[Collector's Address]
[City, State, Zip]

RE: [account number]

Dear [Creditor],

Due to a prolonged period of financial hardship, I have been unable to make payments to you. I am now finally in a position where I can offer you a settlement towards the balance owed in the above referenced account.

Please accept $_____ as settlement-in-full of my debt to you. As part of our agreement, please remove any late payments or charge offs from my credit report.

Please send confirmation of this settlement agreement to the address above. Upon receipt, I will forward you the stated amount within ten days.

Sincerely,

[Your Name]

Example Letter for Countering a Creditor's Settlement Offer

[Date]

[Your Name]
[Your Address]
[City, State, Zip]
Fax [xxx-xxx-xxxx]

[Collector's Name]
[Collector's Address]
[City, State, Zip]

RE: [account number]

Dear [Debt Collector],

I appreciate your willingness to negotiate a mutually agreed upon debt settlement. However the amount you proposed is not feasible for me to pay.

The amount I would be able to come up with, to settle this debt in full, is $_____. I also request that you remove any late payments or charge offs from my credit report.

Please forward a final agreement to me, by mail or fax, if you find these terms and conditions acceptable. Once I receive written confirmation of this agreement from you, I will pay the stated amount within ten days.

Sincerely,

[Your Name]

Example Letter for Acceptance of Settlement (conditional)

[Date]

[Your Name]
[Your Address]
[City, State, Zip]
Fax [xxx-xxx-xxxx]

[Collector's Name]
[Collector's Address]
[City, State, Zip]

RE: [account number]

Dear [Debt Collector],

I have received your proposed settlement agreement and find the settlement amount agreeable. I only ask that you also remove any late payments or charge offs from my credit report.

Please forward a final agreement to me, by mail or fax, if you find these terms and conditions acceptable. Once I receive written confirmation of this agreement from you, I will pay the stated amount within ten days.

Sincerely,

[Your Name]

Example Letter for Acceptance of Settlement

[Date]

[Your Name]
[Your Address]
[City, State, Zip]

[Collector's Name]
[Collector's Address]
[City, State, Zip]

RE: [account number]

Dear [Debt Collector],

I have received your proposed settlement agreement and find the terms and conditions agreeable.

I will forward you the agreed amount of $_____ within ten days.

As part of our agreement, please remove any late payments or charge offs from my credit report.

Sincerely,

[Your Name]

Chapter 9 - How I Eliminated My Debt by Bankruptcy (without an attorney)

Don't forget the Check List (Chapter 16)!

If you have decided to declare bankruptcy, I strongly suggest you educate yourself and speak with a qualified bankruptcy attorney before you decide whether to file your papers yourself. You can find information on the Federal Government's website: http://www.uscourts.gov/bankruptcycourts.html, and on your state's website (Florida's Southern District's is: http://www.flsb.uscourts.gov/. Just search on "bankruptcy in [your state] and you will find good resources and a host of attorneys wanting your money).

Also, if you're even considering bankruptcy, **DO NOT** go out and spend a bunch of money on credit cards. You may be denied a discharge of debts, and may be prosecuted for fraud.

Bankruptcy is something you can do yourself. I did it, and it was a pain in the neck, but it all went ok as I followed the process. You may not want to, because (1) it is an enormous amount of work, and (2) it is a bit complicated.

You have the right to represent yourself. You can save several hundred to several thousand dollars. But unless you do your homework, you may not understand what you need to do in order to get the best results, or to even understand what you are entitled to in the court system. And if you miss a deadline, forget to file the proper forms, or file them incorrectly, you can be denied a discharge or repayment plan or may have to re-file at a later date.

You can also hire an attorney to file your bankruptcy case for you. I suggest you shop around and speak with a few candidates before you hire an attorney. Their rates vary just like any other product or service on the market. To find a local bankruptcy attorney, do a simple internet search on "bankruptcy attorney in [your state or city]".

Please note that child support, alimony, student loans, and taxes are not dischargeable in bankruptcy.

If you are filing for yourself, or if you want to keep up with the process as your attorney files your case, you can follow the process I used as shown in the checklist in Chapter 16. Again, check your state's laws and procedures and speak with an attorney before deciding to do this yourself.

Step One – Decide to Get Out of Debt And Stay Out.

Step Two – Cut Up Credit Cards.

Step Three – Design Monthly Budget.

Step Four – Read "Bankruptcy Basics" (http://www.uscourts.gov/FederalCourts/Bankruptcy/BankruptcyBasics.aspx). They also have videos you can watch on the same Web page. The .pdf version of Bankruptcy Basics can be downloaded or printed by visiting http://www.uscourts.gov/uscourts/FederalCourts/BankruptcyResources/bankbasics.pdf.

Step Five – Reduce Spending On Unneeded Items/Activities.

Step Six – Sell Unneeded Belongings.

Step Seven – Save $1000 Emergency Fund (keep in safe, confidential place).

Step Eight – Downsize (house, cars, etc.)

Step Nine - Decide whether to file yourself or hire an attorney.

Step Ten – Complete Means Test to see which chapter you qualify for. If you plan to file under Chapter 7 you must complete the means test to prove you qualify and that you are not abusing the system. Complete Form B22A, "Statement of Current Monthly Income and Means Test Calculation – For Use in Chapter 7". You can find the means testing Form B22A online by visiting http://www.uscourts.gov/uscourts/RulesAndPolicies/rules/BK_Forms_Official_2010/B_022A_0410.pdf. You have to go to a few different websites and figure out what your state and county's allowances are for food, transportation, etc., as part of the calculation. Don't worry, it isn't that complicated. Just follow the process.

Step Eleven – Complete pre-filing credit counseling (required). To find an approved provider, visit http://www.justice.gov/ust/eo/bapcpa/ccde/de_approved.htm.

Step Twelve – File all statements/correspondence.

Step Thirteen – Decide whether to keep cars with lease or loan payments.

Step Fourteen – Make list of all creditors (Name, address, phone number).

Step Fifteen – Complete Forms to file your case. You can find all the Federal Bankruptcy forms and instructions you will need by visiting http://www.uscourts.gov/FormsAndFees/Forms/BankruptcyForms.aspx.

Step Sixteen - Follow local Court rules for filing. Find your state's website and read every word. The US Bankruptcy Court District in your state will have their own website and administrative rules for filing. For example, the Northern California District US Bankruptcy Court website is: http://www.canb.uscourts.gov/. You must follow local court rules for filing or they will not accept your case.

Step Seventeen – Make three copies of filing package.

Step Eighteen – File case at your local Bankruptcy Court along with the filing fee. The filing fee is usually around a couple of hundred dollars.

Step Nineteen – Notify creditors of bankruptcy case number.

Step Twenty – Complete post-filing financial management course (required). To find an approved provider, visit http://www.justice.gov/ust/eo/bapcpa/ccde/de_approved.htm. **This must be completed before a discharge is granted**.

Step Twenty One – Check credit report and make necessary corrections/repairs (see Chapter 13 of this book).

Step Twenty Two – Rebuild credit (see Chapter 14 of this book).

Step Twenty Three – Monitor Credit Report.

Step Twenty Four – Read IRS Bankruptcy Publication 908 (http://www.irs.gov/pub/irs-pdf/p908.pdf).

Step Twenty Five – Save For Major Contingency Fund (Target $10,000+).

Step Twenty Six – Pay Off Cars (if you kept them) ASAP.

Step Twenty Seven – Pay Off Student Loans ASAP.

Step Twenty Eight – Pay Off Home Equity Loans ASAP.

Step Twenty Nine – Pay Off Mortgage ASAP.

Step Thirty – Borrow To Pay For Things That **APPRECIATE** In Value ONLY.

Chapter 10 - How to Eliminate IRS Debt

The IRS is a special breed of creditor, and you need to play by their rules. Their rules are different than non-governmental creditors, their methods are harsher, and the consequences for defaulting on an IRS obligation are much more painful.

The IRS will accept partial payment, but they make it difficult to obtain a settlement. Their preferred method of taking your money, believe it or not, is convincing you to put the balance on a credit card! For insight into how to pay an IRS debt, straight from the horse's mouth, visit http://www.irs.gov/taxtopics/tc202.html to read IRS Topic 202. It should be no surprise that the federal government recommends going into debt to pay them – they seem to consider debt as a normal part of every-day economics.

If you find yourself in a real bind, and don't feel capable of paying the IRS or don't understand your options, contact a local tax accountant or attorney, or call the Taxpayer Advocate Service at 877-777-4778 or TTY/TDD 1-800-829-4059.

Options for Repaying the IRS

Lump Sum Payment is the easiest, fastest, cheapest, and most pleasant way. If you can do this, then save yourself a bunch of discomfort and do it.

Repayment Plan. For only $45, a steep penalty, and a hefty interest rate, you can set up a repayment plan, if you qualify. Pretty much everyone qualifies. What are they going to do if you don't qualify? I don't know, and I don't think they know either.

Offer-In-Compromise (OIC – the IRS term for settlement) is similar to settling with a credit card company, but you must qualify. The IRS is not as eager to settle with you as credit card companies. Don't let that discourage you – you may indeed qualify and save yourself lots of money by going through the trouble. To see whether you qualify, read the IRS's letter on the OIC process by visiting: http://www.irs.gov/taxtopics/tc204.html and use their OIC Booklet IRS Form 656-B, found at: http://www.irs.gov/pub/irs-pdf/f656b.pdf.

Basically, to qualify, you need to prove that you can't afford to pay the IRS a lump sum or by repayment plan, and:

- Not be in an open bankruptcy proceeding
- Pay the IRS a $150 application fee (unless your income is below their minimum)
- Include with Form 656 a lump sum payment of 20% of your bill, **OR**
- A periodic payment offer

If you don't qualify for an OIC, pay the IRS as fast as you can, by any means possible. You can clean up the mess later. A seasoned tax accountant gave me the same advice, and she was right. I did not qualify for the OIC but was able to pay the IRS by repayment plan, and I paid it as fast as I could.

Default – Prepare for the Levy. The IRS will take money right out of your bank account. If the IRS sees money in your account, and your repayment plan is in default (or was never approved), they'll take that money. You can't do a thing to stop them.

They will even take money out of your joint account with your new spouse if you were divorced and the IRS debt was created while married to a former spouse. The IRS will do this even if your divorce decree requires your ex-spouse to pay the debt - they don't care who was ordered by a District Court to pay them. Your best bet if this happens is to file a lawsuit against your ex-spouse and get your money back.

The IRS will also take your money directly from your employer. It's called garnishing your wages. You are much better off negotiating a repayment plan or OIC than your employer having to collaborate with the IRS to garnish your wages.

Chapter 11 - How to Deal with Creditors and Collection Agencies

Most of the people and organizations you will deal with are surprisingly reasonable and cooperative. Just be honest, friendly, and humble. That will take some of the heat off what would otherwise be an awkward and antagonistic relationship. Their tone may change as your accounts age, but you should keep your cool.

To stop creditor calls, you will have to write them a letter, called a "cease and desist" letter. You have the right to do this under the Fair Debt Collection Practices Act (FDCPA). You can read it or print a copy by visiting: http://www.ftc.gov/bcp/edu/pubs/consumer/credit/cre27.pdf#804. Just telling them over the phone, or ignoring their calls, won't work.

The FDCPA spells out the rules for collectors on harassment, unfair practices, validation of debts, use of deceptive forms, etc. If you ever feel you need to speak with the FTC in person, their number is 877-FTC-HELP.

Example cease and desist letters are provided at the end of this chapter. Use the example letters as a template. Fill in your own information between [brackets] including the current date, your name, address, and account number given by the debt collector.

Another thing you should do when collectors are hounding you is to demand that they validate your debt. By law (specifically, the

FDCPA), a collector has to provide you with proof that they have the right to attempt to collect from you. Example debt validation demand letters are provided for your use at the end of this chapter.

Here is an excerpt from the FDCPA which states the FTC's rules on debt validation, Section 809, Validation of Debts:

> *(a) Within five days after the initial communication with a consumer in connection with the collection of any debt, a debt collector shall, unless the following information is contained in the initial communication or the consumer has paid the debt, send the consumer a written notice containing—*
> *(1) the amount of the debt;*
> *(2) the name of the creditor to whom the debt is owed;*
> *(3) a statement that unless the consumer, within thirty days after receipt of the notice, disputes the validity of the debt, or any portion thereof, the debt will be assumed to be valid by the debt collector;*
> *(4) a statement that if the consumer notifies the debt collector in writing within the thirty-day period that the debt, or any portion thereof, is disputed, the debt collector will obtain verification of the debt or a copy of a judgment against the consumer and a copy of such verification or judgment will be mailed to the consumer by the debt collector; and*
> *(5) a statement that, upon the consumer's written request within the thirty-day period, the debt collector will provide the consumer with the name and address of the original creditor, if different from the current creditor.*
> *(b) If the consumer notifies the debt collector in writing within the thirty-day period described in subsection (a) that the debt, or any portion thereof, is disputed, or that the consumer requests the name and address of the original creditor, the debt collector shall cease collection of the debt, or any disputed portion thereof, until the debt collector*

obtains verification of the debt or any copy of a judgment, or the name and address of the original creditor, and a copy of such verification or judgment, or name and address of the original creditor, is mailed to the consumer by the debt collector. Collection activities and communications that do not otherwise violate this title may continue during the 30-day period referred to in subsection (a) unless the consumer has notified the debt collector in writing that the debt, or any portion of the debt, is disputed or that the consumer requests the name and address of the original creditor. Any collection activities and communication during the 30-day period may not overshadow or be inconsistent with the disclosure of the consumer's right to dispute the debt or request the name and address of the original creditor.

****

Whew! That's a mouthful! Demand debt validation. Once you understand your rights, you can enjoy a little peace of mind in the midst of the storm, and buy some time to prepare for settlements if that's your strategy. You may even stop the collector dead in his tracks!

Send the debt verification demand letters **via certified mail with return receipt requested** so you have proof of the letter's mailing and receipt.

There are other ways of avoiding the constant calls. One way of getting around the nuisance calls is to change your phone number. And prepaid cell phones are a great way to protect your privacy and your personal phone(s) from the barrage of creditor calls. You can pick one up for a few dollars and when you're done with the creditor battles, you can go back to using your normal phone(s).

Changing your phone number may not be convenient for your friends and family. It is probably worth the effort to just write the creditors cease and desist letters. But changing your number or getting a prepaid cell phone also buys you some time and peace of mind. It also helps you save on your phone bills by preventing countless nuisance calls.

TeleZapper is a device that detects when a computer is calling your home phone. When you or your answering machine answer a computer-generated call from a collector, the TeleZapper emits a series of tones that fool the computer on the other end into thinking your phone is disconnected. The collector's computer hangs up and registers your number as disconnected. You can check out more TeleZapper information by visiting: http://www.telezapper.com/.

Telling a creditor you're thinking about bankruptcy does not stop their calls. It does, however, make them more eager to settle your account, and in some cases does slow down the frequency of their calls.

If you are actually declaring bankruptcy, once you get a case number, tell the creditor the case number. They will stop calling you.

If the creditor threatens to file a lawsuit, it's your turn to get eager to settle your account if you are able. Round up as much money as you can – borrow from your family, sell something, whatever you have to do. If you do end up getting sued by a creditor, Chapter 12 of this book will help you deal with the lawsuit.

The fastest and most reliable way to get your correspondence to creditors is to either scan a signed document and email it to them or fax it.

If you don't have a fax machine, there are a number of online solutions that provide you with a way of sending and receiving faxes online. With online faxing, you get a fax number that can send and receive faxes, and you get the faxes as email attachments.

Ring Central (http://www.ringcentral.com/fax/features/how-it-works.html) costs about $8/month for fax services if you sign up for a year. Otherwise, Ring Central costs about $10/month for 500 fax pages. Efax (http://www.efax.com/Free-Trial?VID=36258&TYPE=300087&AID=10596199&PID=4184054) costs about $17/month with a $10 one-time setup charge. MyFax (http://www.myfax.com/index.aspx) also costs about $10/month. This may not be cost effective if you don't plan to fax much, or you would rather mail or scan-and-email back and forth with the creditors. It may be convenient for a month or two, especially if you don't have access to a fax machine. They usually have a 30-day free trial period.

Here is a list of dos and don'ts to keep in mind while dealing with creditors or collection agencies:

DO:
- Mail all correspondence via certified mail with return receipt requested.
- Use courteous, respectful language while speaking (or writing) to creditors. Keep your cool.
- State your situation in simple, brief terms (e.g., you are unable to pay them at this time, or you are interested in settling your account for $xx.xx amount, or you are contemplating bankruptcy, or you have declared bankruptcy and your case number is xxxxxxx, whatever your situation is).
- File all correspondence with creditors for future reference/evidence.
- Mail creditors cease and desist letters to get them to quit calling you.
- Change your phone number or get a pre-paid cell phone.
- Get access to a fax machine or online fax service or scan-and-email correspondence to save time.

DON'T:
- Don't threaten or use vulgar or abusive language.
- Don't let them intimidate you.
- Don't give them any banking or personal information.
- Don't agree to anything over the phone – DEMAND any agreements in writing BEFORE you pay them anything.
- Don't agree to a settlement without the creditor stating, in writing, that your account will be annotated as "Settled In Full" or "Paid In Full".
- Don't get fooled into thinking they will stop bothering you if you just pay them a little bit (no matter what they promise you).

Example Cease and Desist Letter

[*Date*]

[*Your Name*]
[*Your Address*]
[*City, State, Zip*]

[*Collector's Name*]
[*Collector's Address*]
[*City, State, Zip*]

RE: [*account number*]

Dear [*Debt Collector*],

Pursuant to my rights under federal debt collection laws, I am requesting that you cease and desist communication with me, as well as my family and friends, in relation to this and all other alleged debts you claim I owe.

You are hereby notified that if you do not comply with this request, I will immediately file a complaint with the Federal Trade Commission and the [*your state here*] Attorney General's office. Civil and criminal claims will be pursued.

Sincerely,

[*Your Name*]

Example Cease and Desist AND Debt Validation Letter to Collection Agency

[*Date*]

[*Your Name*]
[*Your Address*]
[*City, State, Zip*]

[*Collector's Name*]
[*Collector's Address*]
[*City, State, Zip*]

RE: [*account number*]
Dear [*Debt Collector*],

Pursuant to my rights under federal debt collection laws, I am requesting that you cease and desist communication with me, as well as my family and friends, in relation to this and all other alleged debts you claim I owe.

You are hereby notified that if you do not comply with this request, I will immediately file a complaint with the Federal Trade Commission and the [*your state here*] Attorney General's office. Civil and criminal claims will be pursued.

I also dispute this debt and request proof from you as to its validity. Please forward transaction history and statements from the original creditor, including said creditor's name, address, and contact information to me.

Sincerely,

[*Your Name*]

Example Debt Validation Letter to Collection Agency

[*Date*]
[*Your Name*]
[*Your Address*]
[*City, State, Zip*]

[*Collector's Name*]
[*Collector's Address*]
[*City, State, Zip*]

RE: [*account number*]
Dear [*Debt Collector*],

I am writing in response to a notice received from you on [*date*]. Pursuant to my rights under the FDCPA (Fair Debt Collection Practices Act), I request validation of this debt from your company, which includes the following:

1. Name, address, and phone number of the original creditor.
2. Statements from the original creditor for at least the past twelve months for the above referenced account.
3. A copy of the original signed agreement between me and the original creditor.
4. Proof that your company is authorized to collect this debt on behalf of the original creditor.

If your office fails to respond to my request within thirty days, I will conclude that you waive your claims against me.

Sincerely,

[*Your Name*]

Chapter 12 - How I Dealt with a Creditor Lawsuit (without an Attorney)

Please see my Lawsuit checklist in Chapter 16

I need to start this chapter by repeating that I am not giving legal advice. I can't and won't accept any liability for your outcome if you choose to legally represent yourself in any way. I am sharing my own experience with handling law suits by myself after having received the advice of an attorney and studying my State's statutes and rules of procedure. I am not licensed to practice law, and giving legal advice is considered practicing law. So please read on with the complete understanding that what I am giving you is my story, and not advice. You can do what you want with it.

I do strongly encourage you to contact an attorney if you have any legal questions or need help with any legal issues.

With that in mind, here is what I have learned the hard way by representing myself, also known as going *pro se*, or "for self". Please verify the applicability or validity of this information with your state or county, and please speak with an attorney before entering any legal battle.

The basic aim of a creditor filing a lawsuit against you is this: they want a judge to award them a judgment against you. A judgment is a legal document that legally binds you to pay the creditor a set amount, usually plus interest. If you don't pay them back voluntarily, the creditor can go through a couple more steps and can then take your property and sell it to get their money. Since the sheriff takes his cut of the proceeds, what may be taken from you may be of even higher value than what you owe the creditor in the first place. And since the sale is usually by auction, and the sale price may be a lot less than the "real" value of the property, what they take from you may be **quite a bit more valuable** than what you owe them. If you are already in this situation, or want to avoid it, consider this proverb before you ever borrow money again:

> *Do not be a man who strikes hands in pledge or puts up security for debts;*
> *If you lack the means to pay, your very bed will be snatched from under you.*
>
> *Proverbs 22:26-27*

When I was served with a lawsuit from one of my creditors (see pictures and examples of lawsuit, answer, caption, etc., at the end of this Chapter), the creditor filed a document in court called a Complaint. The creditor was the Plaintiff, and I was the Defendant. The creditor used the Complaint to ask the judge to give them a judgment against me.

I had a limited amount of time to file a formal Answer to the Complaint in the Court. I had twenty days, which is common. If I would not have filed an Answer to the creditor's Complaint, they could have asked the judge for a summary judgment, and I would have lost very quickly. Court procedures allow the Plaintiff to win automatically if the Defendant doesn't make a formal response, or doesn't make the response within the time limit.

By filing my Answer, I was able to delay the process a little while. During that delay, I could have negotiated a settlement and avoided the judgment against me.

The creditor gave me the opportunity to settle out-of-court, even after the law suit had been filed. I didn't have enough money at the time to make a settlement, so the law suit played out and the creditor obtained a judgment against me.

Once they obtained the judgment (the statute of limitations in my state hadn't passed yet, and I did owe them the money as alleged), it showed up on my credit report. They then had the legal right to take my property and sell it to get their money back.

Thinking back on it, knowing what I know now, I should have made a small offer, even if I had to borrow the money. A judgment is not a good thing to have on your credit report, because it shows up on mortgage loan applications, job applications, etc.

I ended up declaring Chapter 7 bankruptcy in the end, and the creditor's judgment against me was discharged (eliminated) in the bankruptcy.

There was never a threat of going to jail – creditors can't put you in jail for not paying them. The judgment and resulting garnishing of wages or confiscation of property are the worst they could have done to me.

The Statute of Limitations for debts is the amount of time, since the last payment you made, that a creditor is allowed to pursue a judgment against you in court. For example, Florida's applicable Statute of Limitations is five years. That means if five years had passed since my last payment was made, the creditor's law suit would have been barred from court by the Statute of Limitations.

This does not mean the debt goes away. After the Statute of Limitations has passed, they can't pursue you in court, but they can still try to collect the debt.

A couple of things to keep in mind about the Statute of Limitations are (1) if I would have made a payment, even a penny, the clock would have started over, giving the creditor another five years to sue me, and (2) if the creditor would have sued me after the Statute of Limitations for my state had passed, I would have been able to use it as a defense, and the case would have been thrown out of court. A table listing the Statute of Limitations, by state, is included at the end of this Chapter.

To file my Answer I needed a formatted document that identified the Court, the Plaintiff and Defendant, case number, etc., and listed my answer to each paragraph of the Complaint.

My Answer had what is called a "caption" at the top of the first page. The caption showed the name of the Court, the name of the Plaintiff(s) and Defendant(s), the type of case, the case number, and the type of filing (e.g., Complaint or Answer).

The body of the Answer contained a paragraph-by-paragraph response to each paragraph in the Complaint. It also listed affirmative defenses, and a brief summary of what I was asking the Judge to do. I was asking the judge to deny and dismiss the Plaintiff's Complaint, and to tax and assess all fees against the Plaintiff.

In my Answer to each individual paragraph of the Complaint, I stated I either Admit or Deny the associated paragraph in the Complaint. At the time I didn't know what I was doing. I should have simply written "Admits" or "Denies" in response to each paragraph in the Complaint, or "Defendant is without knowledge and therefore denies Paragraph X".

My answer also included affirmative defenses. Affirmative defenses are used to address the specific legalities of the creditor's Complaint. For instance, if my state's Statute of Limitations had run out, I could have used that as an affirmative defense. I would have stated that the case is barred from court since the Statute of Limitations has passed.

A note of caution - I cannot properly explain all the available affirmative defenses and when they apply. If you choose not to consult with an attorney, you are using affirmative defenses at your own risk. Due to my lack of experience at the time, the creditor asked the judge for a summary judgment since my affirmative defenses were essentially jabberwocky. The judge agreed and gave them the judgment.

Had I to do it all over again, I would have contacted an attorney, researched my state's statutes and Rules of Civil Procedure to understand my rights and available defenses better, and studied previous similar cases. You can find similar cases online or in a law library. An attorney will usually give you an hour's worth of advice for two to three hundred dollars.

If the creditor had not included evidence in their Complaint, that I really owed them money and the identity of the original creditor, I could have used that as a defense, and the creditor would have had to present such evidence. Had the creditor's Complaint been bogus in any way, I may have won the case.

Here is a bit of personal advice. From my experience, I would have been better off at least paying an attorney a few hundred dollars to look over my Answer and help me with my affirmative defenses, and explain the available strategies and my chances of winning. In my situation, I still would have likely lost the case. It's a judgment call (no pun intended) regarding whether you want to lose a cut-and-dried case for free, or lose it after paying an attorney several hundred or thousand dollars to lose it for you. The best thing to do is ask an attorney if you have any chance of winning before you make that decision.

If I were to file an Answer today, for any type of law suit, I would also consider checking out a very helpful resource like Legal Zoom. Also, county and state courts have self help centers for people representing themselves, and have downloadable forms online.

Here's my strategy for dealing with a lawsuit. You can follow my checklist from Chapter 16 (at your own risk!) and see examples of documents at the end of this Chapter.

Step One – Note the date you are served with a Complaint (Lawsuit) – YOU HAVE 20 DAYS TO ANSWER.

Step Two – Contact Attorney for advice or representation.

Step Three – Contact creditor (or creditor's attorney) and ask for a settlement if you can gather the money to pay it (highly recommended).

Step Four – Check your state's Statute of Limitations.

Step Five - Consult Attorney regarding your defense, especially Affirmative Defenses. Affirmative defenses don't always apply and they require legal experience to use them properly – you are risking your outcome by not consulting an attorney before trying to use them.

Step Six – Write your Answer (if self-representing). See example at the end of this Chapter. Better yet, download a form approved by your local court or check out http://www.legalzoom.com/.

Most courts will require the following sections in an Answer:

CAPTION
ANSWERS TO EACH PARAGRAPH
AFFIRMATIVE DEFENSES
CONCLUSION/REQUEST
SIGNATURE/DATE/ADDRESS (NOTARIZED)
COPIES TO CREDITOR'S ATTORNEY AND DATE SENT.

Step Seven – Make 4 copies of Answer.

Step Eight – Bring original Answer and 3 copies to court clerk. Clerk will keep original. Have clerk stamp 3 copies with the court seal.

Step Nine – Send stamped copy to creditor's attorney.

Step Ten - Wait for notification of pre-trial mediation date or trial date.

Step Eleven – Get one-hour consultation with attorney for advice if you plan to go to court *pro se*.

Step Twelve – Prepare your defense - Short, simple, honest. Be prepared to state reason(s) for financial hardship. Be prepared to offer to make payments for part or all of balance or settlement for fraction of balance.

Step Thirteen – Go to pre-trial mediation if offered. Show up prepared to offer settlement (bring at least 20% of the balance to offer right there).

Step Fourteen – If no mediation offered, go to court.

Step Fifteen – Dress professionally. Speak respectfully to attorneys, judge, and bailiff. Address judge as "Your honor", or "judge". Address attorneys by their last name, "Mr. Last name". DO NOT get angry or emotional. Follow directions – stand when told to, etc. They will tell you what to do. Only answer the questions they ask – DO NOT ramble on and offer information they did not ask for.

Step Sixteen – If you get a judgment against you, either pay your creditor, declare bankruptcy, or hope the creditor doesn't take something from you (not likely, but possible).

Below I show some excerpts of a lawsuit one of my creditors filed against me. I also show portions of a possible Answer, better than the one I originally filed.

Remember, unless you have a really good defense, such as the statute of limitations has passed, or the creditor is committing fraud against you or something, you are probably going to lose the case and get a judgment against you. But filing a proper Answer will at least buy you some time to negotiate a good settlement. If the case was complicated or I thought I had a good defense, I would consult a good attorney for advice, and maybe to represent me.

In my example lawsuit, the creditor offered me an increased credit limit in July, when I was "living on credit cards" due to my impending divorce, attorney bills, etc. I stopped paying them in September. They filed the lawsuit in May of the next year. I had plenty of time to settle with them and avoid the lawsuit, but lacked the money. I didn't know what I was doing, either. At that time I was actually paying a debt settlement service several hundred dollars a month for, well, pretty much nothing. It's clear that their "services" were actually hindering my ability to save enough money to pay a settlement and avoid the law suit.

Knowing what I know today, I would have scraped together every penny I could and settled with them, even if I had to do it after their Complaint had been filed. I hope if you're facing the same situation, you will do what you can to settle with your creditor before it comes to a lawsuit.

John Oswald

Copy of Letter Threatening a Lawsuit (1 page)

March 25, 2008

John J Oswald
6547 Se Federal Hwy Apt 103
Stuart FL 34997-8379

RE: Your account
ending in 4120

Creditor: Chase Bank USA, N.A.

Dear John J Oswald,

Over the past several months you have failed to make the required minimum payment(s) on your above credit card account. As a result, Chase Bank USA, N.A. hereby demands immediate payment of the entire balance set forth above.

If you fail to make payment of the entire balance, Chase has the right to start a lawsuit against you. If a lawsuit is started, you can be served with a Summons and Complaint by a sheriff or process server. The filing of a lawsuit by our attorney starts a series of events that may result in a judgment being entered against you. If a judgment is entered against you, your salary could be garnished.

To avoid a lawsuit, contact one of our representatives at 1-800-327-4676 within fifteen (15) days of the date of this letter to schedule your payment. Otherwise, and without further notice, the bank intends to instruct its attorney to commence legal action against you for the entire balance owed plus appropriate interest and court costs.

If you and Chase agree upon a repayment plan, please remit all promised payments to Chase Cardmember Services, P.O. Box 15905, Wilmington, DE 19886-5905 on or before the agreed date to avoid legal action.

Very Truly Yours,

Chase Collection Support Department
1-800-327-4676

IN-HOUSE COUNSEL FOR CHASE
S.O. DAVIS, CALIFORNIA   S. HARMITT, NEW YORK
A. SHWACHMAN, CALIFORNIA   P. ORSI, FLORIDA
S.A. FAULKNER, ILLINOIS   B.D. LAYTON, NEW JERSEY
M. FINE, ILLINOIS   L.H. FRANCO, NEW JERSEY
T. WILKINSON, NEW YORK

Copy of Lawsuit Filed Against Me (4 pages)

**IN THE CIRCUIT COURT
IN AND FOR MARTIN COUNTY, STATE OF FLORIDA**

CHASE BANK USA, N.A.,

              Plaintiff,

vs.

JOHN J OSWALD,

              Defendant(s).

Case No. **081099CA**
JUDGE ROBERT MAKEMSON

SUMMONS
For Personal Service on Natural Person

THE STATE OF FLORIDA
To Each Sheriff of the State:

    YOU ARE HEREBY COMMANDED to serve this summons and a copy of the Complaint or petition in this lawsuit on the Defendant:

JOHN J OSWALD
6547 SE Federal Hwy Apt 103
Stuart, FL 34997-8379

Dated on: **5/9/01**

NOTICE TO PERSONS WITH DISABILITIES
If you are a person with a disability who needs any accommodation in order to participate in this proceeding, you are entitled, at no cost to you, to the provision of certain assistance. Please contact Clerk of Court's Administration Division, 100 E. Ocean Blvd., Ste. 200, Stuart, FL 34994, 772-288-5576 within 2 working days of your receipt of this document. If you are hearing or voice impaired, call 1-800-955-8771

MARSHA EWING
**CLERK OF THE COUNTY/CIRCUIT COURTS
MARTIN, COUNTY**
LEVI JOHNSON

By: _____
      Deputy Clerk

If you are a person with a disability who needs any accommodation in order to participate in this proceeding, you are entitled, at no cost to you, to the provision of certain assistance. Please contact the Clerk of the Court at 100 East Ocean Blvd., Stuart, FL 34994, 772-288-5576 within 2 working days of your receipt of this notice; if you are hearing a voice impaired, call 1-800-955-8771.

IMPORTANT

    A lawsuit has been filed against you. You have 20 calendar days after this summons is served on you to file a written response to the attached Complaint with the Clerk in this Court. A phone call will not protect you. Your written response, including the case number given above and the names of the parties, must be filed with the Clerk of the Court listed below, if you want the Court to hear your side of the case. If you do not file your response on time, you may lose the case, and your wages, money and property may thereafter be taken without further warning from the Court. There are other legal requirements. You may want to call an attorney right away. If you do not know an attorney, you may call an attorney referral service or a legal aid office (listed in the phone book). If you choose to file a written response yourself at the same time you file your written response to the Court, you must also mail or take a copy of your response to the "Plaintiff/Plaintiff's Attorney" named below.

John Oswald

**IN THE CIRCUIT COURT
IN AND FOR MARTIN COUNTY, STATE OF FLORIDA**

CHASE BANK USA, N.A.,

          Plaintiff,

vs.

JOHN J OSWALD,

          Defendant.

No. 08:1099CA

COMPLAINT

Plaintiff, CHASE BANK USA, N.A. ("CHASE"), a first party creditor, sues Defendant, John J Oswald, and alleges as follows:

1. At all times hereinafter mentioned, CHASE is and was a national banking corporation with its primary place of business located in the State of Delaware.

2. At all times hereinafter mentioned, the Defendant was and is a resident of Martin County, State of Florida.

3. This is an action involving a claim for damages that exceeds $15,000.00.

4. The Defendant had a revolving credit account(s) with CHASE ("the Account(s)") and used the Account(s) to obtain purchases and/or cash advances and, as a result, became indebted to Chase on individual balances for the Account(s) as follows

Account Number	Last Statement Balance
4266841133474120	$ 16352.12
TOTAL:	$16,352.12

True and correct copies of a representation of CHASE's record of the Account(s) is attached hereto as an Exhibit(s).

5. CHASE provided monthly account statements to the Defendant reflecting, among other information, transactions to the Account(s) since the preceding billing period, the total amount due on the Account(s), and the minimum payment(s) due.

6. The Defendant did not object to the aforementioned account statements at any time.

7. The Defendant owes CHASE $16,352.12 that is due on the Account(s) together with interest from May 5, 2008; and costs of suit.

WHEREFORE, Plaintiff, CHASE BANK USA, N.A., respectfully requests entry of judgment against Defendant, John J Oswald, in the amount of $16,352.12, plus interest and costs of the suit.

JPMorganChase-Legal Department
Attorneys for Plaintiff
1191 East Newport Center Drive, Suite 101
Deerfield Beach, FL 33442
954-571-2517

BY: _____
Philip A. Orsi, Esq. / 167177
Lisa Dolin Eiss, Esq. / 0896306
Anthony J. Maniscalco / 548707

John Oswald

Statement for account number: 4266 8411 3347 4120

New Balance	Payment Due Date	Past Due Amount	Minimum Payment
$16,352.12	04/14/08	$1,813.00	$3,451.12

CHASE

Amount Enclosed $ _____ . ____

Make your checks payable to Chase Card Services.
New address or e-mail? Print on back.

4266841133474120003451120163521200000008

0019322XY010005D
JOHN J OSWALD
6547 SE FEDERAL HWY APT 103
STUART FL 34997-8379

CARDMEMBER SERVICE
PO BOX 15153
WILMINGTON DE 19886-5153

:5000 160 28: 203 1133 474 120 7"

CHASE

Opening/Closing Date:	02/21/08 - 03/20/08
Payment Due Date:	04/14/08
Minimum Payment Due:	$3,451.12

CUSTOMER SERVICE
In U.S. 1-800-945-2000
Español 1-888-446-3308
TDD 1-800-955-8060
Pay by phone 1-800-436-7958
Outside U.S. call collect
1-302-594-8200

VISA ACCOUNT SUMMARY   Account Number: 4266 8411 3347 4120

Previous Balance	$15,864.02	Total Credit Line	$16,000
Purchases, Cash, Debits	+$74.00	Available Credit	$0
Finance Charges	+$384.10	Cash Access Line	$3,000
New Balance	$16,352.12	Available for Cash	$0

ACCOUNT INQUIRIES
P.O. Box 15298
Wilmington, DE 19850-5298

PAYMENT ADDRESS
P.O. Box 15153
Wilmington, DE 19886-5153

VISIT US AT:
www.chase.com/creditcards

The charge privileges on your credit card account have been revoked. You no longer have the ability to use your credit card account for purchases. We can help you get back on track. Call 1-800-955-8030 (collect 1-302-594-8200) today.

FLEXIBLE REWARDS SUMMARY

Previous points balance	0
Points earned on purchases this period	0
New total points balance	0
Total points unavailable for redemption	6,819

To redeem your Flexible Rewards points, call 1-800-603-2265, or log on to www.chase.com/creditcards for 24-hour access to your rewards program.

5,469 Points to expire on statement on or after JULY, 2012

TRANSACTIONS

Trans Date	Reference Number	Merchant Name or Transaction Description	Amount Credit	Amount Debit
03/19		LATE FEE		$39.00
02/21		OVERLIMIT FEE		35.00

FINANCE CHARGES

Category	Daily Periodic Rate 29 days in cycle	Corresp. APR	Average Daily Balance	Finance Charge Due To Periodic Rate	Transaction Fee	Accumulated Fin Charge	FINANCE CHARGES
Purchases	V .08216%	29.99%	$5,514.74	$131.40	$0.00	$0.00	$131.40
Cash advances	V .08216%	29.99%	$737.55	$17.58	$0.00	$0.00	$17.58
Convenience check	V .08216%	29.99%	$9,868.04	$235.12	$0.00	$0.00	$235.12
Total finance charges							$384.10

Effective Annual Percentage Rate (APR): 29.99%

Please see Information About Your Account section for balance computation method, grace period, and other important information.
The Corresponding APR is the rate of interest you pay when you carry a balance on any transaction category.
The Effective APR represents your total finance charges - including transaction fees such as cash advance and balance transfer fees - expressed as a percentage.

IMPORTANT NEWS

Take advantage of your points!
Check the top of your statement for your point balance then go to www.chase.com/creditcards to see all of the merchandise, gift cards and travel choices available to you.

EXHIBIT " 1 "

Here is Roughly How I Would Answer Today

(please check with an attorney regarding Affirmative Defenses – there are several you can use, depending on your state and your situation) (4 pages)

IN THE CIRCUIT COURT
IN AND FOR MARTIN COUNTY, STATE OF FLORIDA

CHASE BANK USA, N. A.,

          Plaintiff,

vs.   No. 081099CA

[MY NAME],

          Defendant.

ANSWER AND AFFIRMATIVE DEFENSES

Comes now the Defendant, [My Name], and for his answer to the Complaint filed herein against him, states as follows:

1. Defendant is without knowledge and therefore denies paragraph 1.
2. Admits.
3. Defendant is without knowledge and therefore denies paragraph 2.
4. Defendant is without knowledge and therefore denies paragraph 4.
5. Defendant is without knowledge and therefore denies paragraph 5.
6. Defendant is without knowledge and therefore denies paragraph 6.
7. Denies.

8. Defendant denies each and every allegation not specifically admitted herein and demands strict proof thereof.

WHEREFORE, having fully answered Plaintiff's Complaint, [My Name], *pro se*, respectfully prays that this Honorable Court deny and dismiss same, with all costs and fees assessed and taxed against Plaintiff.

AFFIRMATIVE DEFENSES

Further answering, [My Name], *pro se*, pleads the following affirmative defenses:

9. As his first affirmative defense, Defendant pleads xxxxxxx.
10. As and for his second affirmative defense, Defendant pleads xxxxxxx.

At this point I would consult with an attorney to determine which, if any, affirmative defenses apply and how to plead them. Your Court may not allow them and they may not be applicable to your situation. Here are some examples:

1. *Complaint failed to state basis of claim (either no statute was cited or complaint fails to state facts sufficient to constitute a cause of action as against defendant)*
2. *Plaintiff has failed to mitigate its damages.*
3. *Debt is time-barred: (the statute of limitations has passed).*
4. *Statute of frauds (no contract exists as proof).*
5. *Failure of Consideration: (no exchange of money or goods occurred between the plaintiff and the defendant).*
6. *Lack of Privity: (no relationship exists between you and the collection agency E.g., you never signed a contract or agreement with the collection agency)*
7. *Unclean Hands: (If Plaintiff giving falsified evidence or producing false witnesses)*

And other possibilities:

Lack of jurisdiction over the subject matter; lack of jurisdiction over the person; improper venue; insufficiency of process; insufficiency of service of process; failure to state facts upon which relief can be granted; failure to join a party, etc.

WHEREFORE, having fully answered and affirmatively defended Plaintiff's Complaint filed herein, Defendant [My Name], *pro se*, respectfully prays that this Honorable Court deny and dismiss Plaintiff's Complaint, with all costs and fees assessed against Plaintiff.

_____, Pro Se
My Name
1111 One Way Lane
North South, FL 33333
[phone number]

CERTIFICATE OF SERVICE

I hereby certify that I have this 23rd day of June, 2008, served Philip A. Orsi, Esq., Lisa Dolin Eiss, Esq., and Anthony J. Maniscalco, or JPMorganChase-Legal Department, Attorneys for Plaintiff, 1191 East Newport Center Drive, Suite 101, Deerfield Beach, FL, 33442, with the foregoing Answer by placing same in the U.S. Mail with sufficient postage attached.

_____

June 23, 2008

John Oswald

Copy of Chase's Reply to My Bogus (original) Affirmative Defenses

(they got the judgment as requested) (1 page)

IN THE CIRCUIT COURT
IN AND FOR MARTIN COUNTY, STATE OF FLORIDA

CHASE BANK USA, N.A.,

                Plaintiff,

vs.   Case No: 08-1099 CA

JOHN J. OSWALD,

                Defendant.

REPLY TO AFFIRMATIVE DEFENSES

Plaintiff, CHASE BANK USA, N.A. ("CHASE"), by and through its undersigned counsel, hereby files its Reply to the Affirmative Defenses filed by Defendant, JOHN J. OSWALD, as follows:

1. CHASE denies the allegations of the Affirmative Defenses as alleged in paragraph 8 and requests that said paragraph be stricken in its entirety as it does not contain any valid affirmative defenses.

WHEREFORE, Plaintiff, Chase Bank USA, N.A., respectfully requests entry of judgment against Defendant as sought by the Complaint and for such other and further relief as the Court deems appropriate.

I HEREBY CERTIFY that the foregoing was served by U.S. Mail on June 25, 2008, to John J. Oswald at 6194 C Durham Drive, Lake Worth, Florida 33467.

                                      JPMorganChase-Legal Department/ Attorneys for Plaintiff
                                      1191 East Newport Center Dr., Suite 101
                                      Deerfield Beach, Florida 33442
                                      954-571-2517
                                      BY: _____
                                      Philip A. Orsi, Esq. / 167177
                                      Lisa Dolin Eiss, Esq. /896306
                                      Anthony Maniscalco, Esq./548707

Statute of Limitations by State (years)

AL	6	KY	15	ND	6
AK	3	LA	10	OH	15
AZ	6	ME	6	OK	5
AR	5	MD	3	OR	6
CA	4	MA	6	PA	4
CO	6	MI	6	RI	10
CT	6	MN	6	SC	3
DE	3	MS	3	SD	6
DC	3	MO	10	TN	6
FL	5	MT	8	TX	4
GA	6	NE	5	UT	6
HI	6	NV	6	VT	6
ID	5	NH	3	VA	5
IL	10	NJ	6	WA	6
IN	10	NM	6	WV	10
IA	10	NY	6	WI	6
KS	5	NC	3	WY	10

Chapter 13 - How to Repair Your Credit Report

I hope you haven't already been scammed by one of the companies claiming to be able to repair your credit. You can do it yourself, for free, or for very little cost. Even the Federal Trade Commission (FTC), which governs the credit reporting industry, warns against such scams. The following is an excerpt from the FTC.gov website:

Credit Repair: How to Help Yourself
You see the advertisements in newspapers, on TV, and on the Internet. You hear them on the radio. You get fliers in the mail, and maybe even calls offering credit repair services. They all make the same claims:
"Credit problems? No problem!"
"We can remove bankruptcies, judgments, liens, and bad loans from your credit file forever!"
"We can erase your bad credit — 100% guaranteed."
"Create a new credit identity — legally."
The Federal Trade Commission (FTC) says do yourself a favor and save some money, too. Don't believe these claims: they're very likely signs of a scam. Indeed, attorneys at the nation's consumer protection agency say they've never seen a legitimate credit repair operation making those claims. The fact is there's no quick fix for creditworthiness. You can improve your credit report legitimately, but it takes time, a

conscious effort, and sticking to a personal debt repayment plan.

To read the entire page at FTC.gov, visit: http://www.ftc.gov/bcp/edu/pubs/consumer/credit/cre13.shtm.

The next chapter in this book shows you how to rebuild your credit and improve your credit score. This chapter focuses specifically on cleaning up your credit report. Mistakes or unneeded blemishes on your credit report can hurt your score and your chances of getting loans for legitimate needs (like a home) or even a job.

Your credit report and score are tools. They are used by banks, mortgage brokers, and even employers to judge how well you manage finances, and how much of a risk you are to loan money to. Are you going to default? Are you going to pay on time? Are you dependable and trustworthy? These are all questions that your credit report will be used to answer.

One common problem people emerging from bankruptcy or debt settlement face is that their credit reports frequently show accounts as open and overdue -- when in fact they were closed and the obligations wiped out as part of the bankruptcy or settlement.

If you encounter this, you need to contact the credit bureaus and the lenders and insist that those accounts be properly reported as "included in bankruptcy.", or, "settled in full".

You may have other items listed on your credit report that need to be corrected or removed. One common item worth your attention is *inquiries*. When you apply for credit or someone checks your credit, an inquiry is recorded on your report. Too many inquiries can hurt your credit score. Excessive inquiries tell the potential creditor you might be too eager to get credit or you're having financial problems.

Inquiries stay on your credit report for 24 months. The ones that affect your score the most are those less than 12 months old.

There are two types of inquiries – hard and soft. Hard inquiries, the ones that can hurt your score, are recorded when you apply for credit or a creditor reviews your credit for an application or is trying to collect a debt from you. Soft inquiries don't reduce your score.

They include things like job applications, you request your own credit report, or a utility company reviews your credit.

An unauthorized inquiry must be removed from your credit report in accordance with the Fair Credit Reporting Act (FCRA), Section 604. You need to request the removal of the inquiry (a sample letter is provided at the end of this chapter) and dispute the inquiry with the credit bureau. If the entity that caused the unauthorized inquiry doesn't remove it within 30 days, the credit bureau will remove it for you. The credit bureau has 30 days to investigate your dispute.

If your credit score was harmed by the unauthorized inquiry, you can even sue the creditor for damages.

When you miss payments, go through settlement with a creditor, declare bankruptcy, or whatever, you can expect your credit report and score to be "hurt". But there are black marks on your credit report that may have gotten there by mistake.

Even the credit reporting agencies can make mistakes on your credit report. Creditors can also fail to follow through on their promises to wipe the bad stuff off your credit report. It is important that you look through your credit report and identify anything that doesn't look right.

First let's look at the most common things that mess up a credit report, in their order of "badness":

1. Bankruptcy
2. Foreclosure
3. Repossession
4. Loan Default
5. Court Judgments
6. Collections
7. Late payments
8. Credit Rejections
9. Excessive credit inquiries

Other things that negatively affect your credit report and score are maxed-out credit (your income does not support any more credit), and lack of credit history, especially having no history of rent or mortgage. Let's say you're recovering from bankruptcy and you apply for a mortgage, and you're living with a relative. One reason you might get rejected is because you aren't currently paying rent or a mortgage. The lender calls this "mortgage shock", and may not believe you will be able to handle the added burden in your budget. This happened to me when I applied for a mortgage one year after bankruptcy.

Negative items fall off your credit report over time. Here is how long each item stays on your credit report:

1. Bankruptcy (Chapter 7)   10 years
2. Bankruptcy (Chapter 13)   7 years
3. Judgment   7 years
4. Foreclosure   7 years
5. Collections/Delinquencies   7 years
6. Charge offs   7 years
7. Tax Liens   7 years
8. Credit Inquiries   2 years

The FCRA lays out the rules for credit reporting and is there to ensure your credit report is accurate. It also allows you to dispute items on your credit report that you don't agree with. You can read the pdf version of the FCRA by visiting: http://www.ftc.gov/os/statutes/031224fcra.pdf.

You are entitled to one free credit report every year. The FTC states that www.AnnualCreditReport.com is the ONLY authorized source to get your free annual credit report under Federal law. Other things that entitle you to a free credit report are getting denied credit, unemployment, or if you are on welfare.

In cases where a debt is sold by the original creditor to a debt collector, and the collector tries to collect from you, this may reset the date of last activity, and reset the date of the negative credit report item.

If this happens, you can dispute it, with the credit reporting agency and the collector. Resetting the date of last activity like this is a violation of the FCRA.

To repair your credit report, take the following steps. Example letters are shown at the end of this Chapter.

Step One – Get your credit report from the three major reporting agencies (Experian, TransUnion, and Equifax). Go to AnnualCreditReport.com and order your free credit reports by visiting: https://www.annualcreditreport.com/cra/index.jsp.

Step Two – Read through each report in its entirety. Highlight any item that doesn't seem right or that you don't understand.

Step Three - If anything is not true or is inaccurate, or you don't understand something, find out what it means or why it's on your credit report. Each reporting agency has great information on their website to help you understand the credit report and how to dispute an error or omission.

Step Four – If you determine there is a mistake on your credit report, use the reporting agency's dispute procedure to file a dispute. You can also contact the creditor who reported the mistake or outdated entry and ask them to remove it.

Step Five – Write letters to the reporting agency and the creditor. Include any supporting documentation needed to prove the credit report entry is in error, and send by registered mail, return receipt requested. You can use the example letters, shown below, as templates. Just fill in your own information between the [brackets] and customize to your situation.

The credit reporting agencies have 30 days to resolve the issue. They are required to contact the original creditor and investigate your complaint. If the resolution includes changing your credit report, the agency has to give you a free credit report and an explanation of the dispute resolution.

The original creditor may not be able to even find your files and records within 30 days. If so, they have to remove the item from or fix it on your credit report.

If the item is not resolved to your satisfaction, you can request that a note be placed in your credit report, showing that an item was disputed.

When you write a dispute letter (see the examples below), you can use the following reasons:

- Not my debt
- Item paid or settled in full
- Incorrect original creditor
- Wrong amount
- Incorrect date(s)
- Incorrect status and/or balance
- Charge off date incorrect
- Wrong month on late payment
- Incorrect account number
- Item too old (should have dropped off by time limits)
- Unauthorized inquiry

There you have it. If you do this yourself, rather than hiring a credit fixer to do it for you, you have saved hundreds, maybe thousands of dollars. All the credit fixing company is going to do is write letters, just like I've shown you here. Can you write a letter? Good. Then you can keep your money in your pocket!

Example Letter to Collector to Remove Inquiries

[Date]
[Your Name]
[Your Address]
[City, State, Zip]
Social [xxx-xx-xxxx]

[Collector's Name]
[Address]
[City, State, Zip]

RE: Unauthorized Credit Inquiry

Dear Sir or Madam,
My credit report from [name of credit bureau] shows the following inquiry (or inquiries):

    [Give details of the inquiry or inquiries.]

I did not approve your company to make said inquiry [or inquiries], which is [are] damaging to my credit score. You are prohibited, by Section 604 (1681b(c)) of the Fair Credit Reporting Act, from making such an inquiry without my permission.

I request that you contact the credit bureaus and have the unauthorized inquiry [or inquiries] removed. Please also remove my personal information from your records and notify me in writing when this is done.

Please forward any documentation you may have supporting the authorization of this inquiry [or inquiries] so I may verify its validity.

Sincerely,
[Your Name]

Example Letter to Credit Bureau to Remove Inquiries

[Date]
[Your Name]
[Your Address]
[City, State, Zip]
Social [xxx-xx-xxxx]

[Credit Bureau's Name (e.g. Experian, Equifax, Transunion]
[Address]
[City, State, Zip]

RE: Unauthorized Credit Inquiry

Dear Sir or Madam,
I am writing to request that you correct inaccurate information on my credit report. I recently noticed the following unauthorized inquiries, which have had a damaging effect on my credit score and standing.

- [Describe inquiry number one]
- [Describe inquiry number two]
- [etc.]

[If any of the following is true, state so]

Because of said unauthorized inquiries, I have recently been denied credit. I have attached proof that this was (or these were) an unauthorized inquiry and would like you to remove it from my credit report as soon as possible.

Please ensure the erroneous information, discussed above, is removed from my credit report as soon as possible.

Thank you,
[Your Name]

Example Letter to Credit Bureau (or Collector) to Request Correction to Credit Report

[Date]
[Your Name]
[Your Address]
[City, State, Zip]

Complaint Department

[Credit Bureau or Collector's Name]
[Address]
[City, State, Zip]

RE: Credit Report Dispute

Dear Sir or Madam,
I am writing to dispute the following items in my file and request that you remove them. I have circled the items I am disputing on the attached copy of my credit report. This incorrect information on my credit report has negatively affected my ability to get loans or credit, as well as employment.

The following items [*describe the item, such as a charge off, judgment, etc.*] are incorrect because [*describe why item is inaccurate or incomplete*].

1. Wrong amount listed (put your own reasons here)
2. Information is outdated
3. Etc., etc..

I am requesting that the item (*or items*) be removed (*or request another specific action/change*) to correct my credit report information, and that you forward to me a copy of the corrected credit report once this is done. I also request that these changes be made within 30 days, to avoid any further violation of the FCRA.

Enclosed are copies of [*describe any documentation you are providing as proof – payment records, court documents, etc.*] supporting my request. Please investigate this matter and correct the disputed item(s) as soon as possible.

Sincerely,

[*Your Name*]

Chapter 14 - How to Rebuild Your Credit

We've talked about getting out of debt, and staying out, for thirteen chapters. Why are we going to talk about getting back into debt? We're not, really. Use of credit is not necessarily the same thing as living in debt, and may be wise in certain situations.

You can and should live completely debt free. It's the best way to live, hands down. But for many of us, living in the world we live in, credit is a necessary evil. Our credit "health", made up of your credit report and credit score, is used to judge us and sort us out in many ways. A good credit score may help you land a good job, rent a nice home or apartment, or buy a home with a mortgage. Bad credit may come up during an election if you're running for political office!

If you are in the process of settling debts or declaring bankruptcy, or just getting back on track, you might have noticed your credit score took a nose dive. Can you get it back into the high 700s? Absolutely! You can do it within a few months if you do it right. It depends on how bad your credit score is and what kind of clutter you might have on your credit report. This chapter will help you get your credit rebuilt quickly.

There are several things you can do to improve your credit score. First and foremost is having loans and paying them consistently and on time. Paying rent and utilities on time also has a healing effect on a credit score. Time alone may not cause your score to rise, but it will certainly help your credit report to look better and the things that smashed your credit score (e.g., bankruptcy, foreclosure, charge-off, etc.) will fall off after a while.

The only way to improve your credit score is by the active and responsible use of credit, and the fastest way is to obtain these two types of credit:

- Installment loans: e.g., auto loans, student loans, mortgages, etc.
- Revolving credit: credit cards or home equity lines of credit

There are certain types of loans that do not help your credit score. This is because they are not reported to credit bureaus. An example is a loan taken from your workplace savings plan (i.e. 401k loan).

If you have declared bankruptcy and still have student loans (which typically aren't dischargeable in bankruptcy), or auto leases or loans, you can use them to repair your credit score by paying them on time.

It also helps your credit report and score to pay more than your minimum payment when you can. Besides making payments on time, paying down your existing debt is one of the best ways to improve your credit score. Maxed-out credit has a strong negative impact on your credit report.

After bankruptcy, it is difficult to qualify for an unsecured credit card. An unsecured card is one where you don't need any collateral. The creditor loans you the money purely on the faith that you will pay it back. Even so, unsecured cards can be obtained, and are very helpful in improving your credit score.

Unsecured cards tailored for people rebuilding their credit are expensive because they usually demand hefty processing fees and charge high interest rates. You can avoid the high interest rates by paying your balance in full each month, but the overall cost of using the unsecured card is great. You can rebuild your credit without paying these huge fees.

A great alternative is a secured credit card. A secured card usually gives you a credit limit that equals what you deposit at the issuing bank. Either a secured or unsecured card, post-bankruptcy, typically has a limit of $300 - $500.

Don't go for just any secured credit card. Some secured cards charge huge up-front and annual fees. Find one with the following attributes:

- No application fee
- Reasonable annual fee
- Reports to the major credit bureaus (Equifax, Experian, TransUnion). Your payment history must be reported in order to improve your score
- Becomes an unsecured card after a year or so of on-time payments

Make sure you don't use up more than about 30-50% of your available credit, and pay your balance in full each month. Remember, the best way to rebuild your credit is to sparingly and regularly use your available credit on a credit card.

And contrary to what you may have heard, you don't need to carry a balance or pay interest to build your credit score. The leading credit scoring formulae do not distinguish between balances that are paid off each month and balances that are carried month to month.

You can rebuild your credit without credit cards. It will take a while longer, but may be better for you if you don't trust yourself with a credit card. If you decide to get a credit card, get in the habit of not charging more than you can pay off every month. Do not fall back into the trap of debt.

Depending on your credit history, you may be able to qualify for an installment loan. Some banks will loan you money against a CD. This means you deposit money and purchase a certificate of deposit (CD), and the bank turns around and loans you the same amount. You get to pay it back in payments, and the bank has the money in their hands already, in case you default on the loan. The bank also reports your payment history to the major credit reporting agencies, thus rebuilding your credit.

A mortgage may be within your reach, depending on what landed you in this mess in the first place. It all depends on your score and history.

After bankruptcy, you can get a VA loan in as little as two years, with pristine post-bankruptcy credit history and a history of on-time rent or mortgage payments. If your reason for bankruptcy was outside of your control, you may be approved for a VA loan in as little as one year after bankruptcy.

I tried to get a VA loan, one year after Chapter 7 bankruptcy. I had a good reason for bankruptcy and my credit score was in the mid-700s. I still got turned down, mainly because I didn't have any rent or mortgage history. The bank said I was too great a risk because of potential "payment shock". And not many lenders would even look at my application so soon after bankruptcy.

You can get an FHA loan in as little as two years, with good credit history, post-bankruptcy. FHA loans have interest rates that are usually only half a percentage point higher than regular mortgage rates.

Just ask several lenders what their policies are. Some lenders don't even touch applications with a bankruptcy until three or more years after the bankruptcy.

If you're considering buying a home, make sure you really can afford one. Many people end up declaring bankruptcy because they over extend their finances to buy a home and can't keep up with all the costs of home ownership (e.g., insurance, taxes, repairs, upkeep, utilities, etc).

Also keep in mind today's home mortgage lenders will gladly loan you more than you can afford. Dave Ramsey, author of "The Total Money Makeover", recommends borrowing no more than the amount resulting in a 15 year fixed rate mortgage payment of 25% of your total take home pay.

Let's say you make $80K/year. Your total take home pay is $5,333/month. 25% of that is $1333/month. If you include taxes and insurance in that payment, that much would allow you to borrow, for a 15 year mortgage at 5 percent interest, about $120k. In most cities today, you would have to come up with quite a down payment to get much house for that. It all depends on your tastes and how badly you want to live debt free.

Are you willing to live within your means? Do you want to live debt *FREE*? Then don't over extend yourself to buy your dream home. Bite off only as much as you can chew right now. If you buy a home, make as big a down payment as you can, and pay off the mortgage early if you can.

In summary, use the following tools and strategies to rebuild your credit and improve your credit score quickly:

- use credit sparingly and responsibly
- pay any revolving accounts off each month
- pay rent, utilities, mortgage payments, car payments, child support, etc., **on time**
- choose your rebuilding strategy wisely and save your money – it doesn't have to cost you a fortune to rebuild your credit

Chapter 15 - To Your Freedom (Staying out of Debt)

I get lazy sometimes, especially in areas I think I've mastered. As an example, even though I've written a book about budgeting and managing my credit rating and credit report, I get lazy about it.

Practice what you know. Please don't get lazy about crushing your debt, once and for all, and most importantly, staying out of debt forever. It's not enough to just *know* something. Keep up with your budget. Keep up with your credit report. Teach your children how to properly handle money and stay out of debt. Teach them how to budget. Help a friend or family member get out of debt. Share what you've learned from this book to help people.

> **Borrow money only to pay for things that gain value over time**

From now on, borrow money only to pay for things that increase in value over time. That pretty much narrows it down to a house. And even that may seem like a risky proposition in today's market, wherein home values aren't guaranteed to rise.

Keep in mind that the real estate bubble was created by none other than DEBT. People were encouraged to buy homes they couldn't afford. The Federal Government subsidized the housing markets and ended up crashing them in their zeal to give people something for nothing. That is what debt is, after all - something for nothing. Or so it seems, until it catches up with you and you realize you're chained to it.

Break the chains of debt, once and for all. And if you feel the pull to slip them back on, just for a little while, because you want something NOW and don't want to save up to pay cash for it or admit that you don't really need it, remember this:

> ***The rich rules over the poor, and the borrower becomes the lender's slave***
>
> *Proverbs 22:7*

May God bless you and keep you in His care, in every area of your life, including your finances. I wish you the best in your debt elimination efforts, and would like to hear from you as you progress, and when you break free from the hold of debt. Please visit my website at www.debt-relief-truth.com or email me at debtrel8@debt-relief-truth.com any time, with questions, comments, success stories, or just, "Hi".

Your fellow warrior,

John

Chapter 16 - The Checklists

Use the checklists on the following pages to organize and keep track of your efforts. Don't be afraid to add to them and if you find something is missing or doesn't quite work, email me at debtrel8@debt-relief-truth.com. I welcome any feedback on this book.

Checklists are included for the following:

- Budgeting

- Debt Roll Up

- Debt Settlement

- Bankruptcy

- Lawsuits

John Oswald

BUDGET CHECKLIST

✓	TASK		DUE	DATE COMPLETED
	Discuss the concept of budgeting with your spouse/family		Day 1	
	Start saving receipts for budget design/review (if you use cash)		Month 1	
	Set Goals (dream – don't get hung up on deadlines)		Month 1	
	Add up all monthly incomes		Month 1	
	Add up all monthly expenses	Review credit card and/or debit card and bank statements	Month 1	
		Review receipts (if you've been saving them)		
		Count monthly auto-deductions as expenses (taxes, Ins, 401k, etc.)		
	Subtract monthly expenses from monthly income		Month 1	
	If your budget doesn't show a monthly excess, cut spending to bring budget into balance		Month 1	
	Brainstorm ways cut spending to free up more money for debt elimination and savings		Month 1	
	Plan how much you will spend on discretionary items (dining out, vacations, Christmas gifts, etc.)		Month 1	
	Brainstorm ways to make more money		Month 1	
	Set goals for how to spend, save, and give money in the future		Month 1	
	Discuss your budget with family members and get buy-in		Month 1	
	Create enthusiasm for debt elimination and saving		Month 1	
	Consider using only cash to curb impulsive use of plastic (save receipts!!!)		Month 1	
	Track your budget by tracking all spending		Month 1 and after	
	Adjust budget as you learn or circumstances change		Each month	
	Read "The Total Money Makeover"		Month 1	
	Read "Rich Dad, Poor Dad"		Month 3	
	Read "The Richest Man in Babylon"		Month 6	
	Read "The Greatest Salesman in the World"		Month 9	
	Study personal finance		As time permits	

The Complete Debt Relief Manual

DEBT ROLL UP CHECKLIST

✓	TASK	DUE	DATE COMPLETED
	Decide to Get Out of Debt And Stay Out	Day 1	
	Cut Up Credit Cards (can keep 1 or 2 to maintain credit score)	Day 1	
	Design Monthly Budget	Month 1	
	Save $1000 Emergency Fund	By Month 6	
	Sell Unneeded Belongings	Month 1	
	Reduce Spending On Unneeded Items/Activities	Month 1	
	Downsize (House, Cars, etc.)	Month 1 or ASAP	
	Make Extra Pmts on Lowest Balance Card/Loan Until Paid Off	Month 1 and After	
	Make Minimum Pmts On All Other Cards/Loans Until 1st Paid Off	Month 1 and After	
	Make Extra Pmts on 2nd Highest Balance Card/Loan Until Paid Off	ASAP	
	Make Extra Pmts on 3rd Highest Balance Card/Loan Until Paid Off	ASAP	
	Make Extra Pmts on 4th Highest Balance Card/Loan Until Paid Off	ASAP	
	Make Extra Pmts on 5th Highest Balance Card/Loan Until Paid Off	ASAP	
	Make Extra Pmts on 6th Highest Balance Card/Loan Until Paid Off	ASAP	
	Make Extra Pmts on 7th Highest Balance Card/Loan Until Paid Off	ASAP	
	Make Extra Pmts on 8th Highest Balance Card/Loan Until Paid Off	ASAP	
	Follow Cascading Payoff Until All Cards/Loans Paid Off	ASAP	
	File All Statements/Correspondence	Ongoing	
	Monitor Credit Report	Quarterly	
	Save For Major Contingency Fund (Target $10,000+)	ASAP	
	Pay Off Cars Asap	ASAP	
	Pay Off Student Loans Asap	ASAP	
	Pay Off Home Equity Loans Asap	ASAP	
	Pay Off Mortgage Asap	ASAP	
	Borrow To Pay For Things That **APPRECIATE** In Value **ONLY**	Ongoing	

John Oswald

DEBT *SETTLEMENT* CHECKLIST

✓	TASK	DUE	DATE COMPLETED
	Decide to Get Out of Debt And Stay Out	Day 1	
	Cut Up Credit Cards	Day 1	
	Stop Making **ALL** Credit Card Payments	Day 1	
	Design Monthly Budget	Month 1	
	Open New Savings Account (unrelated to card companies)	Month 1	
	Start Saving At Least 2% Of Total Card Debt In New Account	Month 1 and After	
	Sell Unneeded Belongings	Month 1	
	Reduce Spending On Unneeded Items/Activities	Month 1	
	Change Phone Number	Month 1	
	Save $1000 Emergency Fund (keep in safe, confidential place)	By Month 6	
	Call Original Creditor to Verify Collector's Right to Collect From You	When Contacted	
	Mail Cease And Desist Letters To Collection Agencies	When Necessary	
	Insist On Validation of Debt By Collection Agencies	When Necessary	
	Contact Attorney For Guidance if Threatened With Law Suit	When Necessary	
	File All Statements/Correspondence	Ongoing	
	Inform Creditors of Inability to Pay	Month 1 and After	
	Monitor Credit Report Monthly	Month 2 and After	
	Inform Creditors of Potential Bankruptcy	Month 3 and After	
	Save 25% of Largest Credit Card Balance (Creditor 1)	ASAP	
	Make Settlement Offer (or counteroffer) To Creditor 1	Month 5 or After	
	Insist on Written Terms of Settlement, in proper format	Always	
	Insist on "Paid In Full" or "Settled In Full" posting to Credit Report and request removal of late payments and charge offs from Credit Report	Always	
	Mail Settlement Payments by **REGISTERED MAIL, RECEIPT REQUESTED**, with a copy of the settlement agreement letter	Always	
	Mail Settlement Payments **ON TIME**	Always	
	Pay By Cashier's Check or Money Order From **Non-affiliated** Bank	Always	
	Request settled-in-full or zero balance confirmation letter	1 Week after payment	
	When Creditor 1 Account is Settled, Repeat Process for Creditor 2	ASAP	
	Repeat Process Until All Accounts Are Settled	ASAP	

✓	TASK	DUE	DATE COMPLETED
	Answer Lawsuits As Necessary	<20 Days After Served	
	Declare Bankruptcy **ONLY IF NECESSARY**	When Necessary	
	Repair Credit Report	After Accounts Settled	
	Rebuild Credit	After Accounts Settled	
	Downsize (House, Cars, etc.)	Month 1 or ASAP	
	Save For Major Contingency Fund (Target $10,000+)	ASAP	
	Pay Off Cars Asap	ASAP	
	Pay Off Student Loans Asap	ASAP	
	Pay Off Home Equity Loans Asap	ASAP	
	Pay Off Mortgage Asap	ASAP	
	Borrow To Pay For Things That **APPRECIATE** In Value **ONLY**	Ongoing	

John Oswald

John's BANKRUPTCY CHECKLIST

✓	TASK	DUE	DATE COMPLETED
	Decide to Get Out of Debt And Stay Out	Day 1	
	Cut Up Credit Cards	Day 1	
	Design Monthly Budget	Week 1	
	Read "Bankruptcy Basics" or watch the videos online	Week 1	
	Reduce Spending On Unneeded Items/Activities	Month 1	
	Sell Unneeded Belongings	Month 1	
	Save $1000 Emergency Fund (keep in safe, confidential place)	By Month 6	
	Downsize (House, Cars, etc.)	Month 1 or ASAP	
	Decide whether to file yourself or hire an attorney	Month 1	
	Complete Means Test to see which chapter you qualify for (Bankruptcy Form B22A)	ASAP	
	Complete pre-filing credit counseling	Within 6 months prior to filing	
	File all statements/correspondence	Ongoing	
	Decide whether to keep cars with lease or loan payments	ASAP	
	Make list of all creditors (Name, address, phone number)	ASAP	
	Complete Forms to file your case	ASAP	
	Follow local Court rules for filing (read your state's website)		
	Make three copies of filing package	ASAP	
	File case at your local Bankruptcy Court Along With Filing Fee	ASAP	
	Notify creditors of bankruptcy case number	ASAP	
	Complete post-filing financial management course - **this must be completed before a discharge is granted**	ASAP after case is accepted	
	Check credit report and make necessary corrections/repairs	ASAP	
	Rebuild credit	ASAP	
	Monitor Credit Report	Quarterly	
	Read IRS Bankruptcy Tax Guide - Publication 908		
	Save For Major Contingency Fund (Target $10,000+)	ASAP	
	Pay Off Cars Asap	ASAP	
	Pay Off Student Loans Asap	ASAP	
	Pay Off Home Equity Loans Asap	ASAP	
	Pay Off Mortgage Asap	ASAP	
	Borrow To Pay For Things That APPRECIATE In Value ONLY	Ongoing	

The Complete Debt Relief Manual

John's LAWSUIT CHECKLIST

✓	TASK	DUE	DATE COMPLETED
	Note the date you are served with a Complaint (Lawsuit) – YOU HAVE 20 DAYS TO ANSWER	Day 1	
	Contact Attorney for advice or representation	Day 1	
	Contact creditor (or creditor's attorney) and ask for a settlement if you can gather the money to pay it (highly recommended)	Week 1 - ASAP	
	Check your state's Statute of Limitations	Week 1 - ASAP	
	Consult Attorney regarding your defense, especially Affirmative Defenses	Week 1 - ASAP	
	Write your Answer (if self-representing) CAPTION ANSWERS TO EACH PARAGRAPH AFFIRMATIVE DEFENSES CONCLUSION/REQUEST SIGNATURE/DATE/ADDRESS (NOTARIZED) COPIES TO CREDITOR'S ATTORNEY AND DATE SENT	Week 1	
	Make 4 copies of Answer	Week 1	
	Bring original Answer and 3 copies to court clerk Clerk will keep original Have clerk stamp 3 copies	BEFORE DAY 20	
	Send stamped copy to creditor's attorney	ASAP	
	Wait for notification of pre-trial mediation date or trial date		
	Get one-hour consultation with attorney for advice if you plan to go to court pro se	ASAP	
	Prepare your defense Short, simple, honest Be prepared to state reason(s) for financial hardship Be prepared to offer to make payments for part or all of balance or settlement for fraction of balance	ASAP	
	Go to pre-trial mediation if offered. Show up prepared to offer settlement (bring at least 20% of the balance to offer right there) If no mediation offered, go to court		
	Dress professionally Speak respectfully to attorneys, judge, and bailiff Address judge as "Your honor", or "judge" Address attorneys by their last name, "Mr. last name" DO NOT get angry or emotional Follow directions – stand when told to, etc. They will tell you what to do. Only answer the questions they ask – DO NOT ramble on and offer information they did not ask for	Always	
	If you get a judgment against you, either pay your creditor, declare bankruptcy, or hope the creditor doesn't take something from you (not likely, but possible)	ASAP	

Recommended Reading

The US Bankruptcy Court's publication on Bankruptcy is an excellent compilation of basic information on bankruptcy and can get you pointed in the right direction:

http://www.uscourts.gov/bankruptcycourts/bankruptcybasics.html

Free Means Testing and Affordable Bankruptcy Filing Assistance:

http://www.freemeanstesting.com/zmt/index.asp

Good site for people who want to get help declaring bankruptcy:

http://bridgeportbankruptcy.com/bridgeport/13index.asp

Pre- and Post- Bankruptcy Credit Counseling (required as part of bankruptcy proceedings):

http://www.cccsatl.org/

US Bankruptcy Court's Site (official forms, information, etc.)

http://www.uscourts.gov/bkforms/bankruptcy_forms.html

US Bankruptcy Court's Bankruptcy Abuse Prevention and Consumer Protection Act of 2005 (BAPCPA)

http://www.justice.gov/ust/eo/bapcpa/index.htm

US Trustee's Site (information, links to means testing information, etc.)

http://www.usdoj.gov/ust/

US Bankruptcy Law Official Site:

http://www4.law.cornell.edu/uscode/11/

www.ingramcontent.com/pod-product-compliance
Lightning Source LLC
Chambersburg PA
CBHW030846180526
45163CB00004B/1460